PICTORIAL HISTORY of DUMFRIES

J.A. Mackay

COVER:
Oil Painting of Old Dumfries
by Hugh Rankin

© J.A. Mackay

First Published in 1990
by Alloway Publishing Ltd.,
Darvel, Ayrshire.

Printed in Scotland
by Walker & Connell Ltd.,
Hastings Square,
Darvel, Ayrshire.

ISBN No. 0-907526-45-4

ALL RIGHTS RESERVED

No part of this publication may be reproduced, stored in a retrieval system, or transmitted in any form or by any means without the prior permission in writing of the publisher, nor be otherwise circulated in any form of binding or cover other than that in which it is published and without a similar condition being imposed on the subsequent purchaser.

BIBLIOGRAPHY

Books — *Apostle to Burns: the Diaries of William Grierson* (1981), John Davies; *Bygone Dumfries and Galloway* (4 vols, 1977-9), Desmond Donaldson; *Dumfries' Story* (1988), David Lockwood; *Picture of Dumfries and its Environs* (1832), John McDiarmid; *History of the Burgh of Dumfries* (1906, reprinted 1972, 1986), William McDowall; *Postal History of Dumfries* (1986), James Mackay; *Burns-lore of Dumfries and Galloway* (1988), James A Mackay; *A History of Dumfries and Galloway* (1896), Herbert Maxwell; *Discovering Dumfriesshire* (1989), Andy Murray; *Exploring Scotland's Heritage: Dumfries and Galloway* (1986), Geoffrey Stell; *Dumfries and Galloway: Our Story in Pictures* (1972), James Urquhart.

Newspapers and Periodicals — *Dumfries and Galloway Courier* (1809-84), *Dumfries and Galloway Standard* (1843-), *Dumfries Times* (1833-42), *Dumfries Weekly Journal* (1777-1833), *Dumfries and Galloway Herald* (1835-84), *The Gallovidian* (1899-1949), *Transactions of the Dumfries and Galloway Natural History and Antiquarian Society*.

Directories — *Dumfries and District Directory* (1953-60), *Halliday's Dumfries and South of Scotland Almanac* (1835), *Johnston's Directory of Dumfries, Maxwelltown &c.* (1882-1900), *Pigot & Co's Directory* (1836), *Slater's Directory* (1851).

PICTORIAL HISTORY of DUMFRIES

J.A. Mackay

Alloway Publishing

THE ARMS OF THE ANCIENT
ROYAL BURGH OF DUMFRIES

INTRODUCTION

Not for nothing has Dumfries been dubbed the Queen of the South. This pleasant county town straddling the River Nith — 'Mim-mou'd Meg o' Nith' was how Burns apostrophized it in his electioneering poem "The Five Carlins" — is a douce place by any standards. Today it often has a deceptive air of being a bit of a backwater, and comparatively few of the tourists who drive up the M74 take the trouble to turn off at Gretna and explore the delights of Dumfries and its locality; but this belies its position, historically, economically and geographically. A human settlement for 6,000 years, it played a major role in the development of Scotland from the Middle Ages onwards and has always enjoyed an importance far exceeding its actual physical size. The largest town in the southwest of Scotland between Ayr and Carlisle, it was an important ecclesiastical centre in medieval times, a town of immense strategic importance in the struggle between Scotland and England, and a focal point for a thriving agricultural community.

Dumfries was the first chartered burgh in the region and the only one that continuously maintained its royal status. It has long attracted the favourable comments of visitors, from the time of Oliver Cromwell in the 1650s to the present day. Tobias Smollett, through his character Humphrey Clinker, described Dumfries (1771) as 'a very elegant trading town .... where we found plenty of good provision and excellent wine, at very reasonable prices, and the accommodation as good in all respects as in any part of South Britain. If I was confined to Scotland for life, I would choose Dumfries as the place of my residence.'

I am not a native of the town but I took Humphrey Clinker's advice in 1974 and moved to Dumfries. To me Dumfries is that ideal town — large enough to possess excellent services and facilities, yet small enough to retain a distinctly identifiable character. My home in Newall Terrace is literally a minute's walk from the shops of the High Street, the estimable Ewart Library, the congenial Globe Tavern that was Burns' favourite howff, and the railway station; yet a minute's stroll in another direction brings me to Burns' Walk by the banks of the Nith and thence open countryside. It is possible to walk through the town, down to the Dock Park and along the Nith to Kingholm Quay where ocean-going ships once berthed, or across the 14th century bridge erected by the mother of John Baliol and out into the wilds of Galloway.

Of course, for me a great part of the attraction of Dumfries lies in its intimate association with Robert Burns, Scotland's national bard and the poet of all humanity. The stamp of Burns is all over the town; but who can fail to get a *frisson* as he trudges across the cobblestones of the former Millbrae Loaning (now Burns Street) past the red sandstone house where Burns died in 1796. Burns, in fact, settled in the town in 1791 so, at the time of writing, we are entering upon a Bicentennial Era.

I am very grateful to David Lockwood and the staff of the Nithsdale District Museum for permission to reproduce many of the photographs in this book especially those from the Jean Maxwell collection. To Alistair Cowper and his colleagues in the Ewart Library I am indebted for help with research and the resolution of many of the problems of identification which arose from pictures illustrated here. My thanks are also extended to Ian MacDowall, Morag Williams of the Crichton Museum and the many others who have been of assistance in this project.

Newall Terrace	James A Mackay
Dumfries	1990

HISTORICAL SKETCH

DUMFRIES

The town of Dumfries lies athwart the River Nith on the northern shore of the Solway Firth in the southwest of Scotland. It is situated some 60 miles (97km) southeast of Glasgow and 29 miles (47km) northwest of Carlisle. With a population of almost 30,000 it ranks 24th in the table of the most populous Scottish cities and towns. Its population, in fact, has only increased by 20 per cent in the course of the present century, but its actual area has increased five-fold, so that the density of population has considerably decreased. This was largely achieved in 1929 when the neighbouring burgh of Maxwelltown on the west bank of the Nith voted for incorporation. Subsequently the boundary was adjusted and substantial territory on the west bank of the river was ceded to Dumfries.

BEGINNINGS

The origins of Dumfries are, quite literally, lost in the mists of antiquity. Archaeological evidence that has come to light in recent years reveals that the site of the town was under human occupation as far back as the Mesolithic period (c4000 BC). The first attempts to till the soil and domesticate animals began about 3000 BC and just over a thousand years later the first bronze implements made their appearance in this district. The area was affected by the great Celtic migrations about 600 BC; there are traces of ancient British hilltop enclosures at Wardlaw and Trohoughton on the outskirts of Dumfries and it seems highly likely that a similar site would lie beneath the eminence on which now stands St Michael's Church, with another hillfort located on the mound occupied by Greyfriars Church.

This area, linked by a ridge along which the High Street now runs, stood about 80 feet above sea level and was bounded on the north and west by the curve of the River Nith. On the east and south it was hemmed in by a vast tract of swamps and marshes dominated by the Lochar Moss, the largest tract of wetlands in the South of Scotland until it was drained in the 18th century.

A settlement would have formed naturally in this area where the Nith was both navigable to sea-going vessels and fordable. This was the pattern which governed the siting of such towns and cities as Inverness, Glasgow, Belfast, Dublin and London itself. The name of the town is Celtic, though this is the subject of controversy and several different interpretations. The earliest written reference to the town occurred about 1150 as Dronfres and as late as the early 19th century it was frequently written as Drumfries. The first syllable is a Celtic word (modern Scots and Irish Gaelic *druim*) meaning a mound or ridge which certainly fits the physical description of the place. A generation later (1176) the town was referred to as Dunfres, and later variants of this were Dumfreis, Dumfriese or Dumfries. In this case the first syllable comes from the Celtic *dun* meaning a hillfort, which is quite plausible. The second syllable is generally accepted as coming from the Celtic *phreas* signifying shrubs or brushwood. So we can say that Dumfries means the ridge or hillfort set among shrubs. Far less likely is the explanation that the name denotes the fort of the Frisians, one of the Germanic tribes which made incursions into East Anglia in the 6th century, while the classical *Domus fratrum* (home of the Brothers) is a typical piece of 19th century Romantic fantasy alluding to the Grey Friars of the Middle Ages. Dumfries is unequivocally Celtic, not medieval Latin, in origin.

ROYAL BURGH

It is probable that the town began its identifiable existence as a fortified enclosure on the slight knoll where Greyfriars Church now stands, with a nearby cluster of mud huts above the ford (where Nith Place is now located). Over the centuries the stockade became a stone fort and eventually the castle alluded to in the modern name of Castle Street. Oddly enough, the castle of Dumfries is not among those listed by William the Lion when he declared war on England in 1173, though castles at Lochmaben and Annan (within a 20-mile radius of Dumfries) were mentioned. This does not imply that Dumfries was unfortified at the time; it merely indicates that its fortification was not under royal administration. Galloway, including Dumfries, was then in a transitional state, having only recently ceased to be a separate Celtic kingdom, and was still not fully absorbed into the newly established kingdom of Scotland.

The Gallovidians led by Fergus and his two sons Uchtred and Gilbert, descendants of an ancient Celtic dynasty, were nominally the subjects of the Scottish kings but more often than not were in a state of rebellion against central authority. Successive monarchs - Edgar, Alexander I, David I and Malcolm IV - brought in Anglo-Norman mercenaries to control the unruly Celts from Moray to Galloway and it was left to these incomers to fortify the towns and villages on the fringes of these rebellious districts. These Anglo-Norman families married into the indigenous nobility or absorbed them but did not supplant them. The native Celtic nobles gradually acquired a veneer of Anglo-Norman culture, adopting the dress and the names of the newcomers but often little else.

One such family flourished in the mid-12th century, as the names of Dunegal and his son Ranulf or Randolph occur on several documents of David I and Malcolm IV. Randolph's Anglo-Norman name belied his Celtic origins, but his father belonged to the ancient family of the Dougalls or McDowalls of Galloway which had exerted their patriarchal sway over Stranith (Nithsdale) since time immemorial.

The civic motto *A' Loreburn* alludes to the Lore Burn (variously interpreted as the lower or muddy brook) in line with modern Loreburn Street which formed a natural defence against attack from the east (i.e. the English side of the border). The slogan 'A' Loreburn' was therefore the rallying cry for the burghers to man the defences. A village of mud and wattle huts grew up on the intervening land in the 10th century under the protection of this border fort. The streets on the line of the present Friars' Vennel and the northern end of the High Street and neighbouring Castle Street, with smaller thoroughfares running towards Loreburn Street, and another cluster of dwellings round Nith Place, constitute the oldest part of the town which by the late 12th century had grown to such importance that King William the Lion granted its charter of incorporation as a royal burgh.

William the Lion himself campaigned in Galloway in 1175-6 in an attempt to curb the powers of the rebellious Gilbert and it appears that he made Dumfries his headquarters, as a charter granting land rights to the Bishop of Glasgow was given by the King 'apud Dunfres' at this time. Three subsequent charters of William refer to Dumfries. The first was granted at 'Gretenhou' (Gretna) some time between 1180 and 1188 and mentioned carucates of land in the territory of Dumfries. The second, dating in the same period, is more interesting as it specifically mentions 'that toft at Dumfries which is between the old castlestead and the church', i.e. the piece of land along the High Street between the Castle and what is now St Michael's Church.

However, it is the third charter that is of the greatest significance. Granted at Dumfries itself, it confirmed to the Abbey of Kelso the church of Dumfries 'with lands and tithes of all oblations and the chapel of St Thomas in that burgh'. This chapel, which stood at the head of St Andrew's Street, was named in honour of Archbishop Thomas a Becket, murdered at Canterbury in 1170. Judging by the names of the witnesses, this charter dates between 1183 and 1188. No charter granting burghal status as such exists, but it is obvious that Dumfries had been made a burgh by 1188. We can narrow this down, however, by placing it in the context of the turbulent events of the immediately preceding years.

Following the death of Gilbert of Galloway in 1185 a power struggle ensued between his son Duncan and nephew Roland (heir of Uchtred whom Gilbert had murdered in revolting circumstances a decade earlier). Roland triumphed, but this did not suit either William the Lion or his suzerain, King Henry II (to whom William had done homage at York in 1175 following his disastrous invasion of England the previous year). Henry ordered William to invade Galloway but the expedition failed because Roland effectively blocked the passes leading into his territory. In the summer of 1186 Henry himself, at the head of an army, came up to Carlisle where Roland went to swear fealty. Thereafter Roland accompanied King William, and was one of the witnesses to the charter granted at Gretna. The two charters granted at Dumfries probably date soon afterwards and from this it has been deduced that the elevation of Dumfries to the status of royal burgh must have taken place in July or August 1186.

The development of Dumfries was quite dramatic. Not only did the town obtain the important right to govern itself but it now possessed certain privileges, such as the right to engage in foreign trade, to levy rents and taxes on the burgesses in respect of the land and buildings they occupied, to control the trade and industry within the burgh, to impose fines and tolls, and extract customs duty from the merchants. The grant of burghal status was preceded by the erection of a royal castle on the southern outskirts of the town, a direct outcome of the campaign of 1185. This consisted originally of extensive earthworks, known as Castledykes, but was largely rebuilt in stone 80 years later. The protection of a royal castle stimulated dramatic growth in the last years of the 12th century. Dumfries became the seat of the sheriffdom of Nithsdale where the King's justices came periodically to try cases, impose fines or the death penalty, and give judgment in civil disputes. The common place of execution was a mound on what is now the site of St Mary's Church between the Annan Road and Newall Terrace.

A burgh mill was established on the banks of the Mill Burn, now an underground stream, near the present-day site of the Safeway supermarket, above Nith Place. The parish church, later known as St Michael's after the Archangel who became the burgh's patron saint, was rebuilt at the end of the 12th century. In addition to the Chapel of St Thomas, there was a Lady Chapel and a third, of a more private nature, associated with the new royal castle. The first hospital was erected in this period and stood about a mile south of the market cross.

Obverse of silver penny of Alexander III.

Dumfries was one of the sixteen towns in Scotland (which then included Berwick) to strike coins in the reign of Alexander III. Silver pennies were produced from about

1250 to 1280 by the moneyers Walter and Wilam at a mint which would have formed a part of the royal stronghold at Castledykes. By the middle of the 13th century, the prosperous and rapidly rising burgh of Dumfries had a population of about 2,000. The earliest burgh seal dates from this time and showed the Archangel Michael triumphing over Satan in the form of a serpent. It is not known why St Michael was chosen; but it is supposed that it was derived from the parish church which, in turn, would have been named by the Anglo-Norman lord of the district. Dedications to St Michael were particularly prevalent in areas of Anglo-Norman settlement.

Coat of Arms 1707.

It was at the bustling port of Dumfries that Alexander III mustered his navy for the invasion of the Isle of Man after defeating the Norsemen at Largs in 1263. The ruler of the Sudreys, Magnus Olafson, forestalled invasion by coming in person to Dumfries where he did homage to Alexander. The military importance of Dumfries was strengthened by the erection of the Townhead Mote (on the site of Moat House in Academy Street) and forts on the west bank of the Nith at Lincluden and Troqueer. A stone wall enclosing the town ran along the top of the ditch known as the Loreburn, beginning at the Townhead Mote and running to Sir Christopher's Chapel, then sweeping round the north side of St Michael's Church and terminating on the river bank to the south of Swan's Vennel. Three gates were inserted in this wall: the North Port near the Moat, the East Port near the Chapel and the South Port near the Church, with a fortified gate on the bridge itself. Later three inner ports were added to the defences and were known as the Vennel Port, the Lochmabengate and the Southergate. The memory of the last-named survives to this day in the name given to the southern part of the High Street where it runs into Shakespeare Street.

POWERFUL FAMILIES

The first monastic house was established north of the town, on the west bank of the Nith near its confluence with Cluden Water. This was an area which in centuries gone by had been associated with the Druids whose worship of oak-trees is perpetuated in the name of Holywood. There is to this day a henge or circle of huge standing stones about a quarter of a mile southwest of Holywood parish church, the largest dolmen weighing about 12 tonnes. The Abbey of Lincluden was founded by Uchtred in the mid-12th century and traditionally was the repository of his mutilated body. His grandson Alan (eldest son of Roland) became Lord of Galloway and assured his position by marrying Margaret, daughter of David Earl of Huntingdon and niece of William the Lion. By the end of the 12th century Alan had become one of the most powerful men in the kingdom. When King John invaded Ireland in 1211 Alan furnished a contingent from Galloway and was rewarded with Rathlin Island and extensive lands in Ulster. He was among the barons of England at Runnymede four years later, forcing John to grant Magna Carta.

Lincluden Abbey, from a 19th century photograph.

Although thrice married he had no male issue, so his estates passed to his daughter, the Lady Devorgilla (born in 1213). Originally known as the Lady of Fotheringay (from the Northamptonshire seat of her maternal grandfather, the Earl of Huntingdon), she succeeded her father in 1234 and married John Baliol of Barnard Castle in County Durham. In memory of her dearly beloved husband who died in 1269 she founded Sweetheart Abbey, a few miles southwest of Dumfries and established Baliol College at Oxford; but within the burgh she endowed the Minorite or Greyfriars' monastery which stood at the north end of the High Street. This was a First Pointed edifice, founded in 1262, and comprised an aisled church, a range of cloisters, a refectory and a dormitory.

Devorgilla is also traditionally credited with erecting the first bridge spanning the Nith. This was an immense boon, not only for the townspeople but also for communications between Scotland, England and Ireland, for the trade of the three kingdoms passed that way for centuries. Devorgilla's bridge was destroyed by floods in 1620 but was rebuilt and restored the following year.

Ranulf (or Randolph), of whom we have already spoken, had a grandson Thomas Randolph, brother-in-law of King Robert Bruce and progenitor of the powerful Randolph family. Ruther, a Celtic chief who died in the early 12th century, was the founder of the family of Caer-ruther or Carruthers, still a common surname in the district. King David I gave land near Kelso to another Celt, Maccus son of Unwyn, and from him descended the Maxwells. His grandson, Sir John de Maccuswel, acquired the barony of Caerlaverock, the impressive moated fortress lying to the south of Dumfries. In time the Maxwells became Earls of Galloway and gave their name to baronetcies at Springkell (Dumfriesshire), Cardoness and Monreith (Galloway), Calderwood (Lanarkshire) and Pollok (Renfrewshire), as well as the estate of Maxwelton associated with bonnie Annie Laurie and the burgh of Maxwelltown on the west bank of the Nith.

Celtic and Anglo-Norman families which had early associations with Dumfries include those bearing the names of Crichton, Charteris, Douglas, Scott, Fergusson, Grierson, Moray or Murray, Riddell and Herries. Alan of Oswestry in Shropshire, a Norman knight ennobled by the Conqueror, went north in the 12th century and was the progenitor of the Stewarts who acquired estates in the region, from Garlies in Wigtownshire to Dalswinton near Dumfries.

The Comyns were another Norman family which came to England with William the Conqueror and two generations later moved to Scotland to serve the Anglicizing Kings of Scotland. William Comyn was High Chancellor (1133-42) and engineered the marriage of his nephew Richard to Hexilda, grand-daughter of Donald Bain of the ancient Celtic kings. From this marriage were descended such powerful men as William of Badenoch, Earl of Buchan whose son Alexander married Elizabeth, niece of Devorgilla Baliol. Alexander's cousin was John Comyn the Red, Justiciary of Galloway in the second half of the 13th century. His son, known as John the Black, married Devorgilla's youngest daughter Marjory and thus became brother-in-law of John Baliol.

One of the oldest closes in Dumfries preserves the Comyn connection.

THE WARS OF INDEPENDENCE

Although Dumfries lay within the sphere of the ancient Galloway princes, it came to national prominence at the end of the 13th century. In 1286 King Alexander III was killed in a riding accident at Kinghorn in Fife and was succeeded by his granddaughter Margaret, popularly known as the Maid of Norway. The girl-queen herself died at Orkney in 1290 while on her way to Scotland. This left Scotland without an obvious heir to the throne and led to the competition which was judged by King Edward I of England. Of the contenders, two in particular had strong claims. John Baliol, through his mother Devorgilla, was a great-grand-nephew of William the Lion.

His claim, however, was contested by Robert Bruce, Earl of Annandale, also known as Robert the Competitor who was one generation closer to William the Lion than John Baliol, but descended from a younger daughter. Edward ruled that Baliol being descended from the first born of the family line had the stronger claim to the title. On the death of Alexander III Bruce the Competitor and his son, the Earl of Carrick, attempted to seize the throne in a curious manner. With an armed band they descended on Dumfries and captured the royal castle at Castledykes which was garrisoned in the name of Queen Margaret. This act of rebellion went unpunished; but although he was compelled to recognise the Maid of Norway as rightful sovereign, Bruce was merely biding his time. When Margaret died Bruce was again prevented from seizing the throne which, by the law of primogeniture, Edward I awarded to Baliol in 1292.

Edward took the opportunity to revive the claim of English kings to be suzerains of Scotland and insisted that the successful claimant do homage to him. As both the chief claimants were, effectively, Anglo-Norman barons, the question of homage probably seemed a minor point. Baliol readily conceded, but soon found that Edward meant to exercise much closer control over Scotland than his predecessors. Reviled and derided by his subjects as 'Toom Tabard' (empty coat), Baliol tried to resist his overlord and assert his independence. In 1295 Edward demanded men and money from Scotland for his war with France; instead, King John and his nobles allied themselves with the French. Edward mounted a punitive expedition and defeated Baliol's army at Dunbar. Scotland was put under military occupation and the hapless Baliol was deposed in 1296. The Scots nobility and gentry were summoned to Berwick and forced to acknowledge Edward's supremacy. The list of Scots landowners who swore fealty to Edward is wryly known as Ragman Roll to this day. The first real struggle to re-assert Scottish independence was led, not by the Anglo-Norman barons, but by a democratic body known as the Guardians of Scotland, led by a humble knight, William Wallace of Ellerslie. Edward, 'Hammer of the Scots', counter-attacked, defeated Wallace at Falkirk in 1298 and gradually subjugated the northern kingdom. In the summer of 1300 he besieged Caerlaverock, but shortly before that he captured and garrisoned the castle of Dumfries at Castledykes, adding a tall square stone keep, parts of which remained standing as late as 1719. In June of that year Edward and his entourage lodged in the monastery of the Grey Friars. William Wallace conducted a guerrilla campaign for some time but was forced into hiding, betrayed in 1305 by the treachery of the Earl of Menteith. He was taken in chains to London, tried for high treason and barbarously executed at Smithfield. Scottish morale was at an all-time low and English domination seemed complete.

Early in 1306 the Competitor's grandson, Robert Bruce, Earl of Annandale, was in London, called thither as King Edward's counsellor; but he received a warning from his friend, the Duke of Gloucester, that his life was in danger. Robert Bruce took the hint (in the form of a sum of money and a pair of spurs) and set off immediately for Scotland, his horse shod backwards so that the hoof-prints would throw pursuers off the track. On 4th February he halted at Dumfries where the English justiciars were sitting in assize.

One of these was John Comyn of Badenoch, nicknamed the Red Comyn, whom Bruce encountered in the church of the Minorites. Bruce made an extraordinary proposal to the Red Comyn: 'Take you my lands, and help me to the throne; or else let me take yours and I will uphold your claim.' Faced with such rank opportunism, Comyn refused, with high-minded talk of allegiance to their overlord King Edward. The conversation degenerated into a squabble which ended when Bruce drew a dagger and stabbed Comyn. He rushed out of the church where his friends were waiting and, noting his distraught appearance, asked if anything was amiss.

'I must be off', he replied, 'for I doubt I have slain the Red Comyn.'

'Doubt?' cried Sir Roger de Kirkpatrick of Closeburn, 'I mak siccar!' And with Sir John de Lindsay he rushed into the church and despatched the wounded Comyn. This was one of the most dramatic incidents in Scottish history. Instead of fleeing in blind panic, Bruce and his band of desperadoes rode down to the Castledykes, attacked it in a frenzy and took the garrison completely by surprise. This desperate act on the spur of the moment rekindled the War of Independence that led eventually to victory at Bannockburn eight years later.

But in the immediate aftermath the Scottish cause seemed lost. When King Edward heard of the uprising at Dumfries he was apoplectic with rage and swore to avenge the murdered Comyn. Sir Aymer Valance headed a large army which invaded Scotland soon afterwards and defeated Bruce at Methven near Perth. The English soon recaptured Dumfries and took their revenge by hanging and beheading Sir Christopher Seton, Bruce's brother-in-law who had taken refuge in the castle of Loch Doon on the borders of Galloway and Ayrshire but was betrayed by Sir Gilbert de Corrie. In November 1323 Christiana Bruce, Seton's widow, obtained a charter enabling her to erect a memorial chapel on the site of her husband's execution. Sir Christopher's Chapel of the Holy Rood stood on the Crystal Mount, the location of the present-day St Mary's Church.

BORDER WARFARE

Although a peace treaty between Scotland and England, cemented by the marriage of Bruce's infant son David to Joanna, sister of King Edward III, was arranged at Northampton in 1328 relations between the two countries continued to be turbulent for centuries. The history of Dumfries in this period is one of faltering progress punctuated by continual setbacks. A school was in existence by 1330 and stood near the present-day Burns Statue. The prosperous burgesses built more substantial houses along the High Street, with their yards extending down the slope to Irish Street, and on the west side of St Michael's Street, stretching down towards the Nith. The invasion of Scotland by the party of Edward Baliol in 1332, and their subsequent defeat at Annan, seems to have passed Dumfries by; but after the disastrous defeat of the Scots at Halidon Hill the following year, Edward III invaded Scotland with a huge army and compelled his puppet, Baliol, to surrender a large part of the Border area, including the town, castle and county of Dumfries. Peter Tilliol was then appointed Sheriff of Dumfriesshire and Keeper of Dumfries Castle. Edward III passed through Dumfries in 1334 on his way to subdue Glasgow.

Although much of Scotland remained under English occupation until 1339, the Regent, Robert Stewart, gradually liberated the country. When the Scots were defeated at Neville's Cross in 1346 these gains were lost. From Caerlaverock Edward Baliol devastated Nithsdale and Aymer de Atheles became governor of Dumfries. Edward III again invaded eastern Scotland in 1356 but the scorched earth policy of the Scots denied him an easy victory. The Scots counter-attacked and Sir Roger Kirkpatrick, son of Bruce's abettor in the murder of the Red Comyn, recaptured Dumfries. Ironically this Kirkpatrick was subsequently murdered at Caerlaverock by the son of Sir John de Lindsay.

Dumfries prospered in the twenty years of peace which then ensued (1357-77). On the death of Edward III the Scots, under King Robert Stewart, invaded England in an attempt to regain Berwick, but Henry Percy soon repulsed the invaders. A raid on Penrith by the Earl of Douglas provoked the devastation of Nithsdale by Lord Talbot as a reprisal, but the English were ambushed on their way home laden with booty and slaughtered.

John, Earl of Carrick, changed his name on succeeding his father as King and became Robert III. Almost totally disabled, he left the actual administration of the kingdom to his brother, the Duke of Albany, but it was in his name that Dumfries was granted a new charter on 28th April 1395. Effectively Robert III ratified the existing burghal rights in exchange for a Crown rent of £20 per annum. The Great Chamberlain retained the customs on foreign trade, but the 'petty customs' on domestic goods were to be collected by the burgh chamberlain, along with ground-rents, market dues, court fines and fishing rents which made up the municipal revenue.

Originally the provost and council were elected by the adult male inhabitants as a whole, but by the 14th century the franchise was restricted to the wealthier burgesses. By an Act of 1469, however, election of a new council was restricted to the members of the old council and a representative of each of the incorporated trades. In the course of the 15th century the crafts and trades were systematically organised into guilds, headed by a deacon. In the ensuing centuries, however, the merchant classes managed to hold on to power in the burgh by the simple expedient of having two votes for every one exercised by the trade deacons, and monopolised the office of provost which was not held by a craftsman until the 19th century.

In the 15th century Dumfries suffered from natural disaster as well as the continual enmity between the Scots and the English. In 1439 the plague devastated Scotland. Known as the Pestilence bot Remeid (without remedy), it apparently started in Dumfries, whence it spread to the rest of the country. A period of peace was shattered in 1415 when Archibald Douglas raided Penrith, thus provoking the inevitable reprisals which included the sack of Dumfries. Douglas died in 1424 but his widow, the Princess Margaret, received the lordship of Galloway. On her death in 1440 her remains were interred in Lincluden Abbey and her magnificent, though sadly mutilated tomb may be seen there to this day.

Castledykes was replaced as the principal stronghold by 1442, when we first hear of a Bastille-type of fort in the very heart of the town. The New Wark as it was known was a massive keep with vaulted cellars, used as a prison as well as a castle, and it stood about the centre of the present Queensberry Square. It survived numerous attacks in the next two centuries, but collapsed through neglect and was finally demolished in 1764.

The activities of the Border reivers provided the pretext for an English invasion in June 1449. The Earl of Salisbury with a large army crossed the Solway, seized the castle of Dumfries and ordered the destruction of the town by fire. William, Earl of Douglas and Lord of Galloway, convened a conference of lords and landowners of the Borders at Lincluden in December 1448 for the better defence of the region against English incursion. A peace treaty was negotiated at Durham on 5th November, following the decisive defeat of the English at the battle of Sark (23rd October).

Although Dumfries was now spared the depradations of the English for a number of years, it suffered from the unwelcome attentions of the King of Scots no less. James II led an expedition against the territory of the eighth Earl of Douglas while the Earl and his retinue were visiting Rome. Threave and Lochmaben castles were besieged and Dumfries was occupied by the Royal army. King James later slew the eighth Earl personally, an act which provoked renewed rebellion by his brother, the ninth Earl. In the ensuing campaign Nithsdale and Annandale became the battlefield between the rival factions.

Dumfries even became embroiled in the English civil strife known as the Wars of the Roses. It was here that Warwick the Kingmaker came in 1462 to negotiate an agreement with Mary of Gueldres regarding the marriage of Edward IV. This marriage never took place, but forty years later Dumfries benefitted from another royal union. In 1503 King James IV married Princess Margaret, daughter of King Henry VII. The Union of the Thistle and the Rose brought peace to the Borders. The following year the young monarch visited Dumfries where he presided over a criminal assize in the Painted Hall (where the Burger King restaurant is today), dispensed money to the Grey Friars and worshipped at the Lady Chapel, which then stood on the west side of what is now Irish Street and north of Bank Street, formerly called Calvert's Vennel.

When Henry VIII declared war on France, Scotland, as the ancient ally of the latter, invaded England. At Flodden in Northumberland King James IV and the 'flowers of the forest' were slaughtered. Henry did not press his advantage with a general invasion of Scotland, but let loose large bands of marauders who devastated Annandale and Eskdale.

Marauders of a different breed were the Border reivers who often rustled the cattle on both sides of the frontier. Chief among these was Johnnie Armstrong whom Robert, fourth Lord Maxwell, Lord Warden of the Marches, summoned to a meeting at Dumfries in the autumn of 1525. Armstrong swore submission to the Lord Warden, but continued to rustle cattle. King James V subsequently came to Dumfries, clapped the Lord Warden in jail for neglect of duty and tricked Armstrong into submission near Hawick where he was hanged soon afterwards.

James V again visited Dumfries in 1538. At that time relations between the two kingdoms were rapidly deteriorating, but it is to their credit that the English Privy Council rejected a plan by Sir Thomas Wharton, English Warden of the Marches, to kidnap the Scottish king, although Henry VIII seems to have favoured the plot.

In the summer of 1542 a large English army invaded eastern Scotland, aided by certain disaffected Scottish noblemen, but were checked at Hadden-Rig. Henry VII thereupon declared war and despatched an even larger army, but again the Scots repulsed the invaders at Fala Muir. James V now mounted a counter-attack which failed disastrously at the battle of Solway Moss. The King retired to his palace at Falkland and died soon afterwards. His Queen gave birth to a daughter a week before he died. 'It came with a lass', he said, alluding to Marjory Bruce whose marriage to the Steward of Scotland began the Stuart dynasty, 'and it will go with a lass.'

The lass was Mary, Queen of Scots. Henry VIII tried to pressure the Scots into betrothing the infant Queen to his son (later Edward VI) and sent a large English army to terrorise the Scots into submission. This campaign in the winter of 1543, which the Scots wryly termed 'the Rough Wooing', caused devastation throughout the south of Scotland and once more Dumfries was laid waste. Everything movable was plundered by Wharton's men who then put the town to the torch. Sir Thomas Carleton and an armed band from Cumberland attacked Dumfries in February 1547 and proclaimed the annexation of the town to England. He compiled a list of the burgesses and landowners and forced them to swear loyalty to Henry VIII, but at least the town itself was spared further depradation. When Lord Maxwell and the Laird of Drumlanrig resisted the English in the spring of 1548 the invaders took their revenge by sacking Dumfries. Several hostages, including the warden of Greyfriars, were later taken to Carlisle and hanged there.

THE REFORMATION

The execution of the warden was but the prelude to the suppression of the Grey Friars, in common with the other monastic institutions in Scotland, at the time of the Reformation in 1560. Alexander Gordon of Airds was influenced by the teachings of Wyclif in England and introduced Wyclif's translation of the New Testament to Dumfries. A Protestant group known as the Lollards of Kyle converted a number of the leading families of Nithsdale, but the doctrines of the Reformed Church were first openly preached in Dumfries by William Harlow, an Edinburgh tailor, at 3am on 23rd October 1558 'in the fore-hall of Robert Cunninghame within the burgh of Dunfrese'. This was the same Painted Hall in which King James IV had meted out justice half a century earlier. The burgh magistrates refused to accede to a demand by the

Catholic faction that Harlow be arrested. The actual Reformation in Dumfries, however, appears to have been accomplished without the violence and bloodshed that accompanied it in other parts of Scotland.

On 23rd April 1569 King James VI gave the possessions of the order in Dumfries to the burgh council, in exchange for a promise to maintain Devorgilla's Bridge and a hospital for orphans and the sick poor. The monastery was allowed to fall into disrepair and much of its masonry was later removed in order to rebuild the castle of Dumfries. Part of the refectory continued in use as the kitchen of a tavern in the Vennel until it was demolished in 1876. Sir Christopher's Chapel likewise fell into disuse after the Reformation. The ruin lingered on for more than a century, but in 1715 its stones were utilised in defensive works thrown up during the Jacobite Rebellion.

John Knox himself visited Dumfries in 1562 and presided at the election of a moderator over the various congregations of the district. The candidates were Alexander Gordon (no connection with the aforementioned preacher), lately Bishop of Galloway, and Robert Pont of Culross. Queen Mary, no less, advised Knox against choosing the Bishop whom she dismissed as a dangerous man. The ministers of the district duly elected Pont. In time the Presbytery of Dumfries took over the administrative duties formerly undertaken by the Deanery of Nithsdale. The transition from Catholicism to Presbyterianism was very gradual. In 1575 the Commissioner of Nithsdale to the General Assembly complained that the people of Dumfries persisted in celebrating Christmas which had been banned in 1560.

Queen Mary, brought up in France, returned to Scotland in 1561 after the death of her husband King Francis II. Although by that time the Reformation was an accomplished fact Mary refused to embrace the new faith. Relations between the Queen and her subjects gradually deteriorated over the ensuing six years. On 20th August 1563 Mary visited Dumfries for the first time, ostensibly in connection with the Treaty of Norham which brought peace between Scotland and England, but in fact to intrigue with Sir John Maxwell of Terregles, later Lord Herries, and long-time Warden of the Western Marches. The Queen spent the night at Terregles on the west bank of the Nith about two miles from the town.

The mounting opposition of the Protestant Lords of the Congregation drove the Queen to take action. The Earl of Moray and the disaffected Protestant Lords occupied Dumfries in 1565 and plotted with the English. On 11th October Mary and her consort Lord Darnley visited Dumfries at the head of an army numbering 18,000, well-equipped with siege engines and artillery. Sir John Maxwell, who was swithering between the Queen and the Protestant Lords, threw in his lot with Mary while the Lords of the Congregation fled into England. Maxwell was soon forgiven and even attended the christening of Prince James on 15th December 1566. It was about this time that he was raised to the peerage as Lord Herries. When Mary announced her betrothal to the Earl of Bothwell only three days after the murder of Darnley, Herries is said to have pleaded with her not to ruin her reputation. Be that as it may, Herries served on the jury that acquitted Bothwell of treason, signed a bond approving of the marriage and was one of the witnesses at the wedding ceremony.

At the battle of Langside on 13th May 1568, Herries was prominent in the Queen's army. When Mary fled the battlefield, Lord Herries accompanied her and gave her sanctuary at Terregles on 14th May. The following day she stayed at Dundrennan Abbey in Kirkcudbrightshire, whence it was hoped she would take ship for France; but Mary resolved instead to seek the protection of her cousin Queen Elizabeth of England - a decision which was ultimately to have tragic consequences.

When Mary was imprisoned in England, Lord Herries wrote a strong letter of protest at Elizabeth's treachery. In the autumn of 1568 he went to London to plead his Queen's case in person. Denounced as a traitor, he was arrested on his return to Scotland and imprisoned by order of the Regent Moray, but was released following Moray's assassination in January 1570. A few months later he joined with the Duke of Chatelherault in summoning a meeting of the Estates (Parliament) in the Queen's name. Only six burghs responded, but Dumfries was one of them. When this ploy failed, Lord Herries made every effort at a diplomatic level to secure Mary's release and restoration.

The support of Dumfries for the imprisoned Queen was not lost on the English. Queen Elizabeth retaliated by sending an expedition under Lord Scrope to ravage Dumfriesshire. John, eighth Lord Maxwell (a nephew of Herries) mustered an army, including the burgesses of Dumfries, to resist the invaders. In vain did the burghers try to withstand the cavalry charges of the English army. Augmented by a force under the Earl of Sussex, Lord Scrope renewed his attack and sacked Dumfries. This was the most thorough destruction the town ever suffered. Everything of value was systematically stripped and removed before the town was burned to the ground. Its castle was demolished and its streets reduced to ashes and rubble. Resilient as ever, the townspeople rebuilt better than before. Old loyalties died hard, however, and left a legacy that manifested itself centuries later in sympathy with the causes of Catholicism and Episcopalianism against Presbyterianism, and in a measure of support for the Jacobite movement against the Hanoverian establishment.

FEUDS BETWEEN MAXWELLS AND JOHNSTONES

As the 16th century drew to a close Dumfries and Nithsdale were divided by factions supporting the Maxwells and their deadly rivals the Johnstones. While the Maxwells adhered to the old religion, the Johnstones embraced Protestantism. As usual, however, religion was merely the cloak disguising a plain, old-fashioned struggle for power. Under the encouragement of Lord Maxwell, whose kinsman was provost, Dumfries was rebuilt and its castle was planned on much more elaborate lines than before. The new castle of Dumfries, popularly known as Maxwell's Castle, even incorporated a chapel where Mass was openly celebrated and where Christmas 1585 was the occasion for an enormous gathering. Complaints of popery reached King James VI who visited Dumfries in April 1587 at the head of a large army. As a result, Lord Maxwell was sent into exile and went to Spain where he intrigued with the planners of the Armada. In April 1588 he landed at Kirkcudbright and raised a rebellion in support of the Armada. The castles of Caerlaverock, Dumfries and Lochmaben were garrisoned by Maxwell's supporters. James VI led his army against Dumfries again, but met with resistance from the townspeople, a delaying tactic which enabled Maxwell to withdraw from the castle undetected, though he was later captured near Crossraguel. Caerlaverock capitulated but Lochmaben castle was besieged. When King James borrowed artillery from the English, however, Lochmaben was bombarded into submission. This was not the only co-operation with the English; Maxwell's plot is believed to have been betrayed to the King by English intelligence. James returned to a lukewarm reception in Dumfries and summarily dismissed Provost Maxwell who was subsequently ambushed and slain by a party of Johnstones. The King presided over a court which tried the rebels. Lord Maxwell was imprisoned in Edinburgh Castle but was released as part of a general amnesty celebrating the King's wedding on 12th September 1589.

Maxwell's deadly rival, Sir James Johnstone, did not remain long in the ascendant. In 1589 he plotted with Francis Stewart, Earl of Bothwell (nephew of Queen Mary's third husband) to seize the King. The plot failed and Johnstone was imprisoned at Edinburgh, but escaped and returned to his stronghold at Lochwood. Once again King James led an expedition to Dumfries, but on this occasion he was warmly welcomed, as Lord Maxwell had been restored to the royal favour. James issued a proclamation at Dumfries offering a pardon to those who repudiated Bothwell and agreed to keep the peace.

Sir James Johnstone, however, did not accept the King's offer and his Wardenship was forfeited and given to Lord Maxwell again. This provoked the Johnstones to various acts of lawlessness, culminating in the so-called Johnstone Raid, which ravaged much of Upper Nithsdale in 1592. King James ordered his Warden to punish the Johnstones and they, in turn, formed an alliance with the Scotts, Elliots, Grahams and other Border families and prepared for a showdown. Lord Maxwell mobilised the forces of law and order. About a thousand men were mustered, the largest contingent being the 200 from Dumfries, commanded by Provost Homer Maxwell of Speddoch. A troop of cavalry under Captain Oliphant was ambushed by the Johnstones at Lochmaben; those who escaped the ambush took refuge in the parish church which the Johnstones burned down over their heads.

Steeled by news of this atrocity, the loyal men of Nithsdale marched eastward, crossing the Lochmaben Hills on 6th December 1593 and camping at Skipmyre overlooking the Dryfe Water. It was here the following day that the Johnstones attacked. Maxwell had the larger army, but the ground was not of his choosing and Johnstone was the more skilled tactician. The battle of Dryfe Sands ended in a bloody rout of the Maxwell army and Maxwell himself was slain. Tradition states that the wounded Warden was discovered after the battle by Johnstone's lady who battered him to death with the bunch of massive keys that hung from her chatelaine. Many of the fleeing supporters of Maxwell were cut down by the pursuing Johnstones. Over 700 of the Maxwell faction were killed and many others were mutilated by sword-slashes on the face—hence the expression 'Lockerbie lick' (meaning a face wound) which has passed into the language.

Lord Maxwell was succeeded as Lord Warden by Lord Herries. Johnstone was proscribed as a rebel, but two years elapsed before Herries was strong enough to avenge his kinsman's death. A punitive expedition in 1595 failed abysmally and in desperation King James replaced Herries as Warden in April 1596 by none other than Sir James Johnstone himself, probably reasoning that a position of responsibility might bring the rebel to heel. This ploy failed and after Johnstone had attacked Drumlanrig (July 1597) he was proclaimed an outlaw at Edinburgh. Nevertheless, he was restored to favour in July 1600.

It is small wonder that King James should be impelled to return to Dumfries in force in November 1597. He spent four weeks in the town, dispensing rough justice, hanging the most notorious offenders and taking hostages from the various warring factions. This good work was continued by Lord Ochiltree, whom the King appointed Sheriff, and a further 60 malefactors went to the gibbet. To take the heat out of the situation, King James banished the young Lord Maxwell to Clydesdale, but in 1601 he returned to Nithsdale, hell bent on avenging the death of his father. The Maxwells went on the rampage, which brought King James back to Dumfries, but the King merely re-iterated the banishment to Clydesdale. No sooner had the King departed than Lord Maxwell returned to Nithsdale and resumed his reprisals. He was apprehended and imprisoned at Edinburgh, but escaped in January 1603 and was proclaimed an outlaw. He calmly returned to his estates and was restored to his rank late in 1607. Subsequently he resorted to force of arms to settle a quarrel with the Earl of Morton and was again imprisoned in Edinburgh Castle. Once more he escaped, after making his guards drunk.

When it came to the King's attention that Maxwell was going about Nithsdale openly and insolently, always accompanied by a score of well-armed horsemen, the King ordered Sir William Cranstoune to make a diligent search of Dumfries for the outlaw. Meanwhile Maxwell succeeded in arranging a meeting with his arch enemy, with the avowed intention of slaying him. The meeting took place on 6th April 1608 at Auchmanhill. A quarrel between two of their subordinates a short distance away, leading to an exchange of shots, brought Lord Maxwell and Sir James Johnstone to blows. Maxwell drew a pistol and shot Johnstone dead. For this foul deed Lord Maxwell eventually paid with his own life on the scaffold. At first he fled to France, but in 1612, as he was about to go to Sweden, he was persuaded to return to Scotland and given refuge at Castle Sinclair in Caithness. The Earl of Caithness handed Maxwell over to the King's officers and in due course he was tried, condemned and executed at

Edinburgh on 21st May 1613.

The Globe Tavern, Dumfries, 1859.

WITCH-HUNTS AND RELIGIOUS WARS

King James revisited the burgh in August 1617, fourteen years after he had succeeded to the English throne. Spending the night of 2nd August at Lincluden College, King James entered Dumfries the following day. James found a very different place since his previous visit. During twenty years of peace the burgh prospered and its trade expanded. In addition to the crafts and trades of necessity, such as smiths, wrights, weavers, masons, shoemakers and butchers, the town boasted several glovers, farriers and dyers working in what were then regarded as luxury trades. Dumfries was now the centre of a considerable textile industry. Homespun wool was woven into the hodden grey worn by the common people, or dyed blue and sold as the superior fabric favoured by the upper classes. Appropriately, King James presented the Incorporated Seven Trades with a miniature cannon made of silver, mounted on a carriage of the same precious metal. For some unaccountable reason, however, the cannon was dismounted early in the 19th century and the barrel fitted with a butt which thus transformed it into a musket. In this strange form the Siller Gun has been preserved to this day. The silver cannon was to be the object of annual competition in target practice. This contest took place on a meadow by the Nith, half a mile south of the town and known as Kingholm.

The contest was held each July and became one of the town's chief holidays along with the Riding of the Marches, which took place on the first day of October, and started from the Market Cross or the Whitesands. Both customs died out in the 18th century, but were revived at the beginning of this century.

Near the hamlet of Stoop on the outskirts of the burgh horse-racing was a popular pastime from the late 16th century, and the Town Council provided a silver trophy for this purpose in 1662.

It is believed that James's visit to Scotland in 1617 had as an ulterior motive the conversion of the country from Presbyterianism to Episcopalianism, a form of church government that placed the monarch at its head. The Episcopal party in England used this as the price of their support to the King's plans for effecting the political union of his kingdoms. James refused to summon the General Assembly, but representatives of nine presbyteries met at Aberdeen in defiance of the King. For this, their leader John Welsh was convicted of treason and sentenced to death, but this was later commuted to transportation. Welsh came of an old Galloway family and had attended the burgh school in Dumfries before entering the ministry. Bishops had been part of the structure of church government envisaged by John Knox, but their power was greatly strengthened by King James. In 1616 William Cowper of Perth became Bishop of Galloway, but preferred to reside in Edinburgh, to the neglect of his diocese. The following year, the General Assembly was convened during the King's visit to Edinburgh. James addressed the delegates and told them bluntly: 'The bishops must rule the ministers, as I rule both.' The Assembly of 1618 rubberstamped the King's regulations designed to bring the Scottish church into line with that in England.

This policy was relentlessly carried on by Charles I, after he succeeded his father in 1625. Laud's liturgy, forced on the Scots, smacked of popery and caused the widespread resentment which culminated in the National Covenant, signed on 28th February 1638. Too late, King Charles tried conciliation but the Assembly which met at Glasgow on 21st November was in no mood for compromise; by now the Covenanters were planning military revolt. When the Royal Commissioner, the Marquis of Hamilton, withdrew from the meeting, the Assembly proceeded to excommunicate the two archbishops and six bishops, annulled the Five Articles and the Service-book, and effectively restored Presbyterianism. Provost Corsane of Dumfries denounced Bishop Sydserf of Galloway as a crypto-papist.

General Alexander Leslie, veteran of the Thirty Years War, was recalled to Scotland to command the Covenanting army. The South Regiment, commanded by Thomas, Lord Kirkcudbright, was raised on both sides of the Nith. King Charles sought the support of sympathetic noblemen. The successor to the robber-baron Lord Maxwell was his brother, the first Earl of Nithsdale, a man of great cultural refinement. In January 1639 Nithsdale was ordered to fortify the castles of the area in the King's name. The Covenanters forestalled him and seized Terregles, forcing the Earl to retreat to Carlisle. Though he strengthened the garrisons at Caerlaverock and Threave, he could do nothing about Dumfries whose citizens sided with the Covenanters and occupied the New Wark. In August 1640 the Covenanting army approached Caerlaverock and laid siege. After heavy artillery was brought up the castle surrendered, on 26th September. A Parliament in Edinburgh, summoned by the Covenanters, subsequently deprived the Earl of Nithsdale of the Stewardship of Kirkcudbrightshire, giving this office instead to Lord Kirkcudbright.

The Covenanters now joined forces with the Puritans in England. Following the outbreak of the Civil War in 1642, General Leslie (now Earl of Leven) joined his forces with the Parliamentary army at York. James Graham, fifth Earl and later first Marquis of Montrose, was originally a Covenanter, but his rivalry with the Earl of Argyll led him to change sides. Appointed Lieutenant-General of Scotland by Charles, he invaded Dumfriesshire in April 1644 and entered Dumfries on the 14th, but was forced to withdraw soon afterwards without achieving anything. Dumfries was next occupied by an army of a different character. Following the defeat of the Scots at Dunbar in 1650, Cromwell's troops were at free quarters in the town which suffered accordingly. Following the Restoration ten years later the burgh petitioned the Crown for compensation for damages totalling £2,280, but never received a farthing.

The second half of the 17th century was blackened by the witch-hunts which were prevalent everywhere. There are copious references to witchcraft in the Kirk Session records from the 1650s onwards. This reached its climax after 1656 when the parish minister was required to announce from the pulpit that all persons having evidence to give against those suspected of witchcraft should be ready to furnish it to the Session without delay. In the summer of 1658 a large-scale witch-hunt took place, as a result of which ten women were taken into custody. One was later discharged though banished from the parish, but the other nine were duly convicted on 5th April 1659. Eight days later they were publicly strangled on the Whitesands and their bodies burned at the stake. The burgh records contain the accounts pertaining to the burning of two witches in May 1657. In 1671 eight poor women were charged with witchcraft; two were subsequently put to death in the same cruel manner. There were other cases whose outcome is not clear. Towards the end of the century, however, cases of withcraft were being more leniently dealt with. According to McDowall, the last case in Scotland was tried at Dumfries in 1709 when Elspeth Rule was found guilty of witchcraft and suffered the penalties of banishment and burning on the cheek with a red-hot iron. The last witch burned at the stake, however, was the unfortunate woman who suffered this barbarous penalty at Dornoch, Sutherland in 1720 after having been found guilty of changing her daughter into a pony, shod by the Devil.

On his Restoration in 1660 Charles II determined to turn back the clock and restore Episcopalianism to Scotland. James Sharpe was soon appointed Archbishop of St Andrews. A specially selected Parliament met at Edinburgh in January 1661 and duly approved a series of measures which effectively destroyed democracy in religious and secular matters. On 16th April 1661 the Convention of Burghs sent instructions to Dumfries, purging the Town Council of Whigs who refused to take the new oath, and replacing them by ultra-Royalists. The majority of councillors refused at first to accept these terms, but eventually most of them gave way. The Trades, however, were less compliant. They numbered in their ranks many men of independent mind who later joined the ranks of the Covenanters, but for the time being they were forced to recant publicly and promise to be more circumspect in future.

The Rev. Hugh Henderson, minister of Dumfries, was ejected in October 1662 for his attachment to the Covenant, 'to the grief and sorrow' of the Council who petitioned in vain for his re-instatement. Heavy fines were imposed for non-conformity; those who protested at the new forms of worship were banished. Rioting and demonstrations were answered with shows of force and troops of dragoons were sent to keep the people in order. A commission appointed by the Privy Council sat at Dumfries in May 1663 and led to the conviction of the ring-leaders. Passive resistance thereafter manifest itself in absenteeism from Episcopal services, punishable by heavy fines. This exacerbated the resentment of the people and brought the Southwest of Scotland to the brink of insurrection. Field-preachings, known as conventicles, spread rapidly and for their protection the worshippers armed themselves.

To crush such rebellious behaviour the standing army was increased in size and placed under the command of Sir Thomas Dalziel of the Binns. His chief lieutenant was Sir James Turner whose troops roamed at will, exacting imposts on the non-conformists and taking up free quarters, looting and pillaging and generally terrorising the populace into submission. This oppressive behaviour reached its peak in November 1666 when Turner's troopers confiscated the crops of an old man named Grier at St John's Clachan of Dalry. They had stripped him naked and were about to torture him with a red-hot gridiron when a group of Covenanters, who had sought refuge in the village, accompanied some of the villagers to restrain the soldiers. The troopers drew their swords and wounded two of the villagers, but they were eventually overpowered. Fearing reprisals from the garrison at nearby Balmaclellan, the Covenanting group decided to attack. The soldiers were taken by surprise, one was killed and the others captured. In this casual manner the Covenanters' rebellion began in Galloway.

The following day a Covenanting force of 200 infantry and 50 cavalry mustered under the command of Andrew Gray at Irongray, six miles from Dumfries. Before dawn on 15th November this little army marched on Dumfries, reaching the Brigend by 8am. They were amazed to find the bridge unguarded and entered the town unopposed. While the infantry waited on the west bank the cavalry rode into Dumfries. Sir James Turner was still abed when he was awakened by the clatter of hooves in the High Street. One of his men was killed in the ensuing fracas, while Turner and the others were quickly overpowered and disarmed. Turner was paraded half-naked through the town on a low nag for the derision of the populace. The Town Council dissociated themselves from the revolt and sent Bailie Stephen Irving to Edinburgh to report to the Privy Council. The insurgents marched back into Galloway with their prisoners. When news of the outbreak reached Edinburgh the Covenanters there decided to rise in support. The result was the ill-fated battle of Rullion Green on 28th November when the rebels were overwhelmed by a large army led by Dalziel. Many others were executed in the aftermath. Two of the fugitives from the Pentland Rising returned to Nithsdale but were afterwards apprehended, tried and sentenced to death. They were duly executed and their heads and right arms were displayed on the Bridge-Port. The obsequious Council (1668) required the inhabitants of the burgh to sign a declaration detesting the late rebellion. Those who refused to sign were heavily fined.

The Earl of Lauderdale appointed a commission to investigate Sir James Turner's behaviour. When he was found guilty of numerous excesses he was cashiered. The Government tried to win over the people by a more conciliatory approach, by relaxing the ban on Presbyterian ministers; but at the same time other, more repressive measures were enacted to cowe the populace. The conciliatory approach failed, when it was perceived as part of the Declaration of Indulgence which removed the restrictions on Catholics at the same time.

In 1675 the Maxwells' castle in Dumfries was considerably strengthened and garrisoned by fifty foot and twelve cavalry. This measure, however, did not deter the Covenanters whose conventicles were better attended than ever. As time passed, opinions hardened and polarised. Isolated acts of rebellion led to deliberate outrages on both sides. The hated Archbishop Sharpe was assassinated on Magus Moor, St Andrew's on 3rd May 1679 and less than four weeks later an armed band entered Rutherglen, extinguished the bonfires celebrating the anniversary of the King's Restoration, and burned the Acts establishing Episcopacy. John Graham of Claverhouse, who had been appointed commander of the dragoons in the southwest, took rigorous measures to root out armed conventicles. His troopers came upon one such field-preaching at Cumberhead near Lesmahagow, but were driven off in disarray. This was the first round in a campaign that led to victory for the Covenanters at Drumclog on 1st June and encouraged their march on Glasgow. They were halted at Bothwell Bridge and sustained such a defeat that their cause seemed doomed. Nevertheless, exactly one year later, an armed band led by Richard Cameron entered Sanquhar and published their manifesto denouncing the King.

The 1680s were later known as the Killing Times. Cameron and his followers were defeated at Airdsmoss, but individual Covenanters were mercilessly hunted down and often shot on the spot. For eight years Claverhouse and his colleagues in persecution went about their repressive work. Chief among the local collaborators was Sir Robert Grierson of Lag whose townhouse in Dumfries was for long afterwards regarded with fear. Many are the cairns on lonely moorlands and the plaques and inscribed slabs in kirkyards all over Nithsdale that testify to the atrocities perpetrated against the Covenanters in this period. James Kirko of Sundaywell was actually shot on the Whitesands in June 1685, and a granite memorial marks the spot.

After the death of Cameron in 1680, leadership of the extreme Covenanting sect known as the Cameronians devolved on James Renwick of Moniaive, one of the most fearless of the field preachers. Despite the most rigorous attempts to track him down, Renwick eluded capture till January 1688 when he was caught in Edinburgh. He was executed on 17th February, the last martyr for his faith. King James VII and II, who had succeeded his brother Charles in 1685, was a Catholic and lost no time in publishing an edict of toleration. This ought to have taken the heat out of the bitter sectarianism of the time, but instead it was perceived as paving the way to a Catholic takeover, and was thus strenuously resisted by Protestants of all shades of opinion. A curious outcome of this edict was the appointment, in January 1687, of John Maxwell of Barncleugh, a confirmed Catholic and kinsman of the Earl of Nithsdale, as Provost of Dumfries. Before he could be re-elected at Michaelmas 1688, however, the Bloodless Revolution had replaced James II by William of Orange. On Christmas Day the townspeople celebrated the downfall of King James with a huge bonfire fuelled by all the Catholic vestments and figures of the saints and Virgin Mary they could lay hands on, together with an effigy of the Pope. In their zeal they also tore down the carved woodwork from the upper storey of Maxwell's Castle where Mass had been celebrated. The hapless ex-provost was arrested and sent as a prisoner to Edinburgh, under guard of none other than Grierson of Lag, erstwhile persecutor of the Covenanters but now ingratiating himself with the new regime!

The Presbyterian form of church government was restored on 15th August 1689, after a gap of 26 years, the Rev George Campbell being appointed minister of Dumfries in place of the curate Richard Brown.

NATURAL DISASTERS AND STEADY PROGRESS

By 1600 the population of Dumfries had risen to about 4,000. Its relatively slow growth in three centuries may be accounted for by the long succession of Border wars which took a heavy toll on the inhabitants. Natural disasters, however, also played their part in regulating the population. The harvest failed in 1598 over the whole of Scotland and many people, in Dumfries as elsewhere, starved to death as a result. Weakened by famine, the populace were unable to withstand an epidemic of bubonic plague the following year. Kirkcudbright Town Council noted (20th April 1599) that 'the pest being verie ill in Drumfries' communication with that burgh was banned for the time being. Famine and pestilence returned to Dumfries in 1623. In the first ten months of that year 492 people died in the burgh; ominously, no records were kept for the remaining two months. When the Great Plague hit London in 1665, the Town Council of Dumfries set up a body of 24 men to keep a round-the-clock vigil against travellers or merchandise from south of the Border, let alone from the affected metropolis.

Disaster of another kind struck at regular intervals as, sadly, it continues to do to this day. The Nith habitually burst its banks when spring tides combined with periods of torrential rain to put the river in spate. Great hardship was occasioned by these floods, but in 1620 the Nith came down with such force that it destroyed Devorgilla's bridge. Even at that time the main commercial traffic of three kingdoms passed over the bridge and its destruction materially affected the commerce of Ireland and England as well as Scotland. This was emphasised in the petition of the Council for Government aid. The Government refused to help but permitted the Council to apply to fellow councils for assistance. Sad to relate, the appeal to other burghs fell on deaf ears. The original piers survived and at least a portion of the arches; about half of what is now extant would have been the original erected in the 14th century. Rebuilding commenced as soon as possible and was completed the following year.

Much of the stone used in the rebuilding came from a new quarry at Castledykes which also provided the characteristic red sandstone in which Dumfries was now largely rebuilt. This quarry resulted in the beautiful sunken gardens that now form a part of Castledykes public park. After the Restoration there were many improvements in the public buildings of the burgh, notably in St Michael's Church (1666) and the erection of a meal market on a site north of the Tolbooth.

St. Michael's Church in the 1980s.

Progress in communications with the rest of the country made a quantum leap in September 1642 when a regular weekly postal service between Carlisle and Portpatrick was established, with links to London and Ireland. Post offices were opened along this route, and Robert Glencors, merchant burgess of Dumfries, was appointed postmaster with responsibility for the mails between Dumfries and Annan. A regular weekly foot-post between Dumfries and Edinburgh was established in December 1664. This became the responsibility of William Fingass, a prominent local innkeeper who was Dean of the burgh in 1675-6, Bailie from 1676 to 1685 and latterly Commissioner to the Convention of Burghs in Parliament.

After the Revolution Dumfries regained its prosperity and grew dramatically. The population in 1700 exceeded 5,000.

The tavern kept by Bailie Fingass - or rather his wife - stood on the prominent site now occupied by Burton's. Most of the Council business was conducted there, rather than in the Tolbooth nearby. The latter had been erected in 1481 on the site of the old Deanery, on the east side of the High Street, and was substantially rebuilt in 1627. To the north was the burgh prison, built in 1579, but the Tolbooth also contained a small lock-up under the external staircase which gave access to the Council chamber on the upper floor. The Tolbooth had a suite of cellars and four shops on the ground floor.

In 1697 the lease of the Customs and Foreign Excise of Scotland was auctioned off to the Convention of Royal Burghs for £33,300. Each burgh was offered a share in the venture and Dumfries subsequently disposed of its share to Robert Dickson of Inveresk and John Sharpe of Hoddam. When news of this reached the ordinary people of the town there was a great outcry and the inhabitants sued the Council with a view to having the deal nullified. Eventually Sharpe suggested a compromise, as a result of which the matter went to arbitration. Finally it was agreed that Dickson and Sharpe could retain their bargain provided they paid 20,000 merks into the burgh purse. This windfall was applied to the erection of a building that would be both an ornament and serve a useful purpose. The result was the Mid Steeple, built in 1707 to the design of Thomas Bachup of Alloa. Essentially this was a council chamber occupying an upper floor and approached by external stairs, with a prison below and a fine clock-tower and steeple above. The total cost of this building, the town's principal landmark to this day, was about £1,500.

Up to 1707 the burgh mills relied on horse-power, but in 1705 the Council authorised the erection of a water-mill on the west bank of the Nith. This served the additional purpose of diverting a considerable flow of water away from the Dumfries side of the river and therefore lessened the proneness of the Whitesands to flooding. The new town mill came into operation on 27th October 1707. To facilitate this project the Council purchased a strip of land on the west bank running south from the Brigend, and on this they built a road leading to the mill. Up to that time only a solitary house stood at the western end of the bridge, but in no time at all drying kilns and housing for the millers were erected. This cluster of dwellings was known as Brigend and became the nucleus of Maxwelltown. To regulate the river still further a mill-dam, known to this day as the Caul, was erected. It ran diagonally across the river from the Mill Green to the Whitesands and effectively prevented the tidal waters from getting farther north while, at the same time, providing a cascade that greatly improved the appearance of the Nith. The Caul was partially destroyed on four occasions - in 1742, 1800, 1820 and 1867. Each time the damage was caused by icebergs brought downstream after a thaw and pressing against the submerged wall.

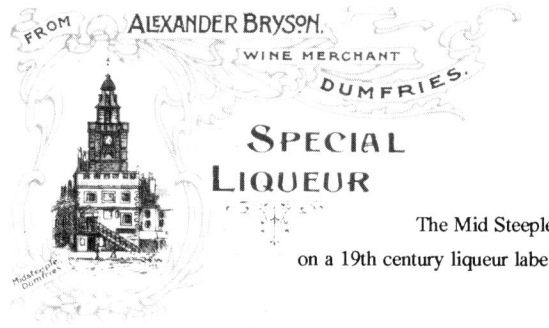

The Mid Steeple, on a 19th century liqueur label.

POLITICAL UPHEAVALS

King James VI's dream of uniting his dominions politically was not realised till almost a century later. Although The Act of Union in 1707 eventually had a beneficial effect it was, at the time, viewed with hostility and suspicion, not the least by the Presbyterian ministers who were afraid that the position of the Church of Scotland would be undermined. The General Assembly, meeting in Edinburgh in October 1706, counselled the Scottish Parliament against anything that might destroy the privileged position of the Church.

On 20th November the 40th anniversary of the capture of Sir James Turner was celebrated in dramatic fashion when about 300 Cameronians rode into Dumfries, lit a bonfire at the Cross and burned the Articles of Union. More ominously, a document listing that 'parcel of rogues in a nation' - the Commissioners who had signed the treaty ending Scottish independence - was also consigned to the flames, with the cry 'Thus may all traitors perish!' The demonstrators disappeared as rapidly as they had come, but rumours that up to 7,000 men had assembled under arms reached Edinburgh and alarmed the Duke of Queensberry, the chief Scottish architect of the Union. Interestingly, an account of the burning of the Articles of Union was subsequently printed. It is believed that this document was printed locally, although the earliest printing press of which record survives was that operated by Peter Rae a few years later. The first book he printed was, appropriately, *A History of the Late Rebellion* (1718).

The Union of Scotland and England was achieved without further mishap and soon its material benefits were being felt. The Scots were now allowed to trade freely with the English colonies in America. Although Glasgow was the main beneficiary of this, Dumfries shared in this prosperity and its little seaport flourished. Not all of the trade was legitimate by any means; the heavy duties on imported articles encouraged smuggling all along the Solway coast. A Custom-house was erected at Dumfries by 1710 and its staff were charged with the surveillance of the Galloway coast, but they were too few in number to prevent the illegal trade.

The death of Queen Anne, last of the Stuart dynasty, in 1714 and the accession of the Elector of Hanover encouraged the supporters of the Old Pretender (the son of King James VII and II) to try and recover the throne. The Earl of Mar, dismissed from office by King George I, was the leader of the movement known as the Jacobite Rebellion. Under cover of a hunting party, the leading Jacobites gathered in August 1715 and the Stuart standard was raised on the Braes of Mar. Many of the Catholic noblemen and gentry of Nithsdale were implicated in the uprising; but the Whig faction, which included former Covenanters, took measures for the defence of Nithsdale and received the full support of the Town Council of Dumfries. The district was defended by the trained bands, including seven companies of 60 men (representing the Seven Trades) and a body of young men known as the Company of Loyal Bachelors, all under the command of Provost Robert Corbet.

William, fifth Earl of Nithsdale and William, sixth Viscount Kenmure raised the Jacobite standard in the Borders and Cumbria. On Saturday 8th October news was brought that the Jacobites were planning to attack Dumfries the following day (Communion Sunday). This was treated as a hoax, but the guards were strengthened and the inhabitants put on the alert. The following day, a Jacobite force consisting of 153 horse commanded by Kenmure rode down from Moffat with the intention of seizing the burgh, but on learning that the town was armed to the teeth, Kenmure withdrew his men. Several hostages were taken when they went out to monitor the movements of the Jacobites and included Bailie Paterson, the postmaster John Johnston and a surgeon named Hunter. They were later released in exchange for some Jacobite sympathisers who had been imprisoned in the town. A curious aspect of this episode was that Simon Fraser, Lord Lovat, suddenly turned up at Dumfries, on his way from London back to his estate near Inverness. The wily old fox claimed to be a loyal supporter of King George. He even offered to lead a party of troops to ambush the Jacobite force which, by now, had withdrawn to Lochmaben, but he was refused permission - a wise decision in retrospect, for Lovat turned out to be one of the Jacobite leaders! Within a month the Jacobite cause had petered out in England and thereafter the menace of attack receded. The battle of Sheriffmuir on 22nd December was inconclusive but by February 1716 the rebellion had fizzled out. The Earl of Nithsdale was sentenced to death but on the eve of his execution at London he made a dramatic escape from prison, disguised as his wife's maidservant, and died an exile at Rome in 1744. Viscount Kenmure, however, was beheaded.

While the Lord Lieutenant, William Johnstone, first Marquis of Annandale, organised the heroic defence of Dumfries, his brother John planned to attack Dumfries on behalf of the Jacobites. He was arrested and imprisoned in the Tolbooth before he could do any damage and was released when the affair was over. In 1730 he wrote an effusive letter of thanks to the Town Council for having saved him from actions that might have lost him his head.

Thirty years later, however, Dumfries was embroiled in the Jacobite rising in favour of Prince Charles Edward Stuart, the Young Pretender, who landed at Moidart, Inverness-shire on 25th July 1745. The chief support of this rebellion came from the Highland clans, while, on this occasion relatively few of the Jacobite and Catholic gentry of the Lowlands gave their assistance. The only gentleman of note in Nithsdale to join the Jacobite army was James Maxwell of Kirkconnell near New Abbey. While General Sir John Cope marched north in search of the Prince's army, the latter advanced on Edinburgh unopposed. Following Jacobite victory at Prestonpans the rebels advanced into England. They got as far as Derby before they ran out of momentum and began their inevitable retreat north. On their way south the division commanded by the Duke of Perth had passed through Nithsdale. The Town Council ignored two demands for money sent by Prince Charles. Injury was added to insult when a party of Dumfriesians cut off part of the Jacobite baggage train near Lockerbie.

For these reasons, therefore, the Jacobites singled out Dumfries for severe treatment on their retreat north. The main body, some 4000 strong, headed by the Prince and the Duke of Perth, advanced on the town. On Friday 20th December 1745 the advance guard of 500 cavalry commanded by Lord Elcho entered Dumfries unopposed. Provost Bell was taken hostage to ensure the good behaviour of the town and the Council was compelled to negotiate with John Hay, appointed Regent by Prince Charles. The Jacobites demanded £2,000 and 1,000 pairs of shoes, together with all the arms and ammunition in the burgh, the total to be surrendered within 24 hours. The Council managed to raise £1,195 by the due time. The burgh was scoured for shoes, but only 255 pairs could be found. The Highlanders were quartered on the unwilling townspeople and indulged in some looting of shops and private houses. Prince Charles himself lodged in the Blue Bell Inn (later the County Hotel) near the foot of the High Street. The large room in which he held court was afterwards preserved as Prince Charlie's room - until the Hotel was demolished in the early 1980s.

News of the imminent approach of the Hanoverian army led by the Duke of Cumberland, however, came late on the Sunday night. The report was a trifle premature, but it had the desired effect. The Jacobite army left Dumfries on Monday morning, taking ex-Provost Andrew Crosbie of Holm and Walter Riddell of Glenriddell as hostages for the delivery of the money and shoes in full. They were not set free till the Jacobites reached Glasgow and the balance of £805 due from Dumfries had been paid. In April 1750 the Government re-imbursed the town by £2,848 5s 11d (from the forfeited estate of Lord Elcho) for the money and shoes, but the total loss incurred by the burgh had exceeded £4,000.

The visit of the Young Pretender was the last incursion of a warlike nature to affect Dumfries. In the ensuing half century the burgh prospered as never before. The mercantile progress was greatly assisted by improvements in the navigation of the Nith and the erection of a proper port at Glencaple, six miles south of the town. Lesser port facilities also existed at Kelton and at Kingholm, which today serves as a harbour for pleasure craft. Glencaple quay was built in 1747 and a picturesque village sprang up soon afterwards. The first cargo unloaded at Glencaple (15th May 1747) consisted of Maryland tobacco, brought aboard the ship *Success* owned by ex-Provost Crosbie, Prince Charlie's erstwhile hostage.

In the town itself the recreational area along the Nith known as the Dock was laid out with about 80 oak saplings supplied by the Duke of Queensberry at Drumlanrig, a notable benefactor to the burgh till his death in 1778. In the 1830s the oaks, by then much reduced in number, were augmented by over 100 lime trees. Moorheads' Hospital (the gift of James and William Moorhead) 'for decayed burgesses and destitute orphans' opened in 1753. The third Duke of Queensberry who did so much to promote the interests of Dumfries during his tenure of the title (1711-78) was commemorated by the public square laid out in his honour and for many years dominated by a Doric pillar. In the 1930s the Queensberry monument was relocated in front of the County Buildings, but in 1990 it was to be restored to its original site. The Duke took an active interest in the replanning of Dumfries which took place from 1752 onwards. Existing streets were improved and lit, while new streets were created. Sometimes, however, the Council's ambitions overran their slender resources and they were forced to sell valuable assets to relieve their debt. The coffee house and news-room in the High Street adjoining the Council chambers were disposed of in 1753.

Burgh politics were extremely lively in the second half of the 18th century and the debates between the Pyets and the Corbies (pigeons and crows) as the opposing factions were nicknamed often became very heated, even to the point of violent scenes of mobbing and rioting in and around the Council chamber. During the burgh elections of 1759 several bailies and councillors were kidnapped and illegally detained. As a result of this, twelve men were arraigned at the High Court in Edinburgh on charges of riot and tumult. This shameful episode came to an end the following year with the election of Robert Maxwell of

Cargen as provost, an office which he held, off and on, till 1781.

Dumfries in 1790.

Rioting was by no means an uncommon occurrence in the 18th century. In February 1771 there was an acute shortage of meal in Dumfries and the mob plundered the burgh granaries and mills to prevent the exportation of grain to other parts of the country. Two of the ring-leaders were subsequently transported to the American colonies and several others were imprisoned. A similar outbreak occurred a few years later, Laghall farm being plundered and farmers prevented from loading grain on to vessels anchored at Kingholm Quay. On this occasion, however, the provost summoned troops who opened fire and killed one of the rioters. During the funeral procession (which passed by the provost's shop in the High Street) the mourners took the opportunity to use the coffin as a battering ram against the shop door. Further 'meal riots' occurred in March 1796, July 1826 and - worst of all - in July 1842. These ugly incidents were generally provoked by shopkeepers sharply increasing the price of meal or bread in times of drought and shortage. In the rioting of 1796 Maxwell Hyslop, youngest son of Burns's friend William Hyslop, was beaten within an inch of his life by the rabble. In the 1842 rioting hundreds of people went on the rampage through both Dumfries and Maxwelltown for upwards of twelve hours and five bakers' shops were attacked and looted during the disturbance.

Associated with Dumfries was William Paterson, born at Skipmyre a few miles to the east. The projector of the ill-fated Darien Scheme (in which several burgesses speculated heavily), he is best remembered nowadays as the founder of the Bank of England in 1694 and the Bank of Scotland a year later. Little more than a century later the Rev. Henry Duncan of Ruthwell founded the world's first savings bank and is remembered affectionately in Dumfries as the 'Stane Man' (from his statue that adorns the facade of the Trustee Savings Bank in Academy Street to this day). The town's association with banking, however, was not always so felicitous. In 1769 the Ayr Bank was founded by Douglas, Heron & Company. Its growth was meteoric, a branch was opened in Dumfries and many of the developments of the period were funded by loans from the bank. The bubble burst in 1772 and triggered off a general panic which devastated the economy of Southwest Scotland for more than a generation. Many of the leading citizens of Dumfries, from Provost Hepburn downwards, were hard hit and several were completely ruined. Dumfriesshire provided a third of the shareholders and a quarter of the bank's capital, so the crash hit the area very hard.

Trade was just beginning to recover when the American War of Independence erupted in 1776. Dumfries was not as hard hit by this conflict as the great mercantile ports, such as Glasgow, Liverpool and Bristol, though the knock-on effect must have been substantial.

In the year that the war ended David Staig was first elected provost. He held office continuously until 1817 and for more than forty years exerted a prodigious influence in the burgh as agent of the Bank of Scotland. Under his enlightened and energetic administration Dumfries got its first paving, cleansing, lighting and police, followed by sweeping reform of the municipal revenues (1788). The first regular mail-coach service (1789) resulted from his persistence and initiative, but his crowning achievement was the laying down of Buccleuch Street and the erection of the New Bridge (1790-2). The Theatre Royal, now Scotland's oldest provincial theatre, was proposed in 1790 and opened in 1792.

ROBERT BURNS

Scotland's national poet Robert Burns first visited Dumfries in June 1787 when he was made a freeman of the burgh. Little did he realise then that he would spend the last four and a half years of his tragically short life in the town. After a two-year sojourn in Edinburgh where he was lionised by the literati he settled to a life of farming at Ellisland combined with a career in the Excise. The fatigue of trying to improve the unrewarding soil of Ellisland and riding 200 miles a week on surveying duties was too much for his far from robust frame. In November 1791 Burns and his family moved into the town and took up residence in an upper-floor apartment in the Wee Vennel above the Stamp Office. In May 1793 the Burns family moved to a more commodious house in the Millbrae Loaning (now Burns Street) and it was here that he died on 21st July 1796. Over a hundred poems and songs were composed - a sixth of his total output - in the Dumfries period. Burns took a keen interest in burgh politics and wrote a series of ballads for the General Election campaign of Patrick Heron (formerly of the notorious Ayr bank) in 1795. He was closely associated with the formation of the public library in 1792, as well as a co-founder of the Theatre Royal. A staunch advocate of the principles of liberty, equality and fraternity, he estranged many of his friends by his outspoken views on the French Revolution which erupted in 1789; but towards the end of his life he was among the first to enrol in the Royal Dumfries Volunteers, one of the numerous militia units raised in response to the threat of French invasion. His funeral on 25th July 1796 drew the largest crowds ever witnessed in Dumfries. His widow, Jean Armour, continued to live in Burns Street till her death in 1834. The burgh abounds with memorials to Burns. His remains were transferred to a neo-classical Mausoleum in 1817 and a statue opposite Greyfriars Church was erected in 1882. Plaques commemorating him may be found in St Michael's Church and on the outer wall of Loreburn Church, on the Theatre Royal and on the two houses in which he lived (the latter being preserved as a museum). The old Town Mill was converted into the Robert Burns Centre in 1986 and is now one of the burgh's most popular attractions.

Burns's funeral procession.

NINETEENTH CENTURY DEVELOPMENTS

The long period of the French Revolutionary and Napoleonic Wars, stretching from 1793 till 1815, benefitted Dumfries by and large. The town became temporary home to several regiments at various times. This influx stimulated trade, while the officers had a refining influence on the burgh's social life. The Theatre got off to a flourishing start and many famous actors and actresses performed there to capacity audiences. During the summer the Dumfries and Galloway Hunt and the Caledonian Hunt held race meetings on Tinwald Downs east of the town; in the winter months the fine Assembly Rooms in Irish Street witnessed many a ball and soiree. During the spring and autumn court circuits the fashionable and well-to-do of the surrounding countryside flocked to the balls and exhibitions held in the town. A burgeoning interest in gardening led to the foundation, in September 1812, of the Dumfriesshire and Galloway Horticultural Society. The informal meetings and dinners of the Burns Mausoleum Committee led to the institution of the Dumfries Burns Club in 1820 - merely the first of many clubs and societies devoted to the memory of the Bard which eventually flourished in the burgh. In 1834 the windmill on Corbelly Hill, the most prominent landmark in Maxwelltown since its erection in 1730, ceased operation. It was purchased by the Astronomical Society, a group of gentlemen who transformed it into an Observatory, complete with camera obscura. This, in turn, became the nucleus of the present burgh museum which was taken over by the local authority in 1934.

Dr James Crichton, briefly a surgeon in the employment of the Honourable East India Company but for most of his career a merchant in Canton and Macau, retired to Scotland where, in 1809, he purchased Friars' Carse. He married Elizabeth Grierson, heiress of Lag but died childless in 1823. Dr Crichton left £100,000 to be spent on some charitable project. At first the Crichton trustees planned to establish a university in Dumfries, but on this being opposed by the four existing Scottish universities, the trustees put the money to an equally worthy use. Forty acres of land at Mountainhall, south of Dumfries, were purchased and an impressive Italianate structure was built in 1838-9. This was the Crichton Institution, designed as a mental hospital. From the outset, this was a model for the treatment of mental illness on the most enlightened and humane lines, very much ahead of its time. It was originally intended for private patients, but the Southern Counties Asylum was added in 1848 for poor patients. As the Crichton Royal Hospital, it remains in the forefront of the treatment of mental illness to this day and a pioneer in geriatry and the rehabilitation of alcoholics and drug addicts. In view of the fact that the good doctor made his fortune peddling opium to the Chinese, there is an element of poetic justice in this.

In the early years of the 19th century Buccleuch Street, running east from the New Bridge, and Castle Street, running at right angles to the top of it, were laid out with fine buildings. The genteel nature of this part of the town was marred, however, by the relocation of the burgh jail midway down the south side of Buccleuch Street in 1807, especially as it was then - and for many years thereafter - the custom to hang convicted felons publicly on the street in front. Five executions took place in the space of six years (1820-6). Thereafter Dumfries was remarkably free of such gruesome spectacle. After the jail was rebuilt on a grander scale in 1851, however, the scaffold was erected twice. In 1862 Mary Timney was publicly executed for the murder of Ann Hannah and on 12th May 1868 Robert Smith paid the supreme penalty for the rape and murder of 11 year-old Thomasina Scott. These were the last female and male public hangings to take place anywhere in Scotland.

Until the late 18th century Dumfries had grown little in size since the Middle Ages and, as a result, many of its vennels and loanings had degenerated into overcrowded slums. To ease this congestion feus were taken in areas to the east of the Loreburn and to the south of St Michael's. The main development took place in Brigend, which had become a bustling town in its own right, with a population of almost 2,000 by 1800; but it was beyond the jurisdiction of the Town Council and the lawlessness of its inhabitants was proverbial, thanks to the London magistrate, Sir John Fielding who stated that Metropolitan detectives could trace a thief over the entire kingdom if he did not get to the Gorbals of Glasgow or Brigend of Dumfries. This appalling state of affairs was remedied in

1810 when Philip Forsyth of Nithside obtained a charter erecting it into a burgh of barony under the name of Maxwelltown and became its first provost. The illicit whisky stills and thieves' kitchens were soon dealt with and a newly respectable Maxwelltown began to attract considerable industry, notably two iron foundries, a sawmill and extensive woollen mills. On the Dumfries side of the Nith new housing was erected at Whinnyhill, but the biggest development took place on the edge of Lochar Moss where Joseph Gass laid out the village named Gasstown in his honour.

Further public works and improvement schemes might have been feasible, had not the burgh got itself into serious debt. Bad management of the municipal revenues in a period of economic growth had left the burgh indebted to a number of individuals and institutions. The parlous state of the burgh finances came to light in 1816 when the treasurer resigned and it was found that he had borrowed £1,500 which he was unable to repay. A panic ensued, during which a number of prominent creditors called in their loans. In order to avoid bankruptcy the burgh was forced to sell some of its assets, including the lands of Kingholm and Milldamhead. The crisis was narrowly averted, but of course the long-term damage was incalculable. The value of these lands rose sharply and the town was commensurately deprived of substantial revenue in the form of the rents which would otherwise have been payable.

Despite these setbacks, the burgh continued to undertake a number of improvements and extensions to the civic amenities. The cattle market on the Whitesands was enlarged and paved in 1821, the New Assembly Rooms were erected in 1825 and gas-lighting was provided to the principal streets in 1826. There was even cash to spare for luxuries, such as new clocks for St Michael's and the Mid Steeple (1821) and a gold chain of office for the provost (1822). The Dumfries and Maxwelltown Mechanics' Institute was founded in March 1825 and inaugurated a year later. It provided the first impetus to adult education and boasted a fine library numbering over 8,000 volumes, subsequently transferred to the Ewart Library following its opening in 1903.

Attempts were made in 1823 to improve the navigation of the Nith, so that large vessels could come up-river as far as Dockfoot. The river was dredged and its rocky bed blasted. Tall embankments were built on either side and a massive harbour wall at Dockhead, but problems with the capricious tides of the estuary made ships' captains prefer to berth at Glencaple or Carsethorn. The commerce of the Nith went into irreversible decline in the middle of the century, with the coming of the railway.

Inevitably many of the old landmarks of the burgh were destroyed in the course of the re-developments that took place between 1780 and 1850. These included the New Wark which had been partially demolished in 1737 and converted into tenement dwellings. This crumbling eyesore was finally razed to the ground in 1846 to make way for Queensberry Square. The townhouse of Sir Robert Grierson of Lag, known as the Turnpike, was demolished in street-widening operations.

The Turnpike House about 1730.

The leading hotel in the early 19th century was the King's Arms, the Whig headquarters at election-time. One of the oldest hostelries in the burgh, and the most fashionable in its heyday, it had been a favourite resort of the Town Council and a place frequented by Burns the Exciseman while attending official dinners. Its chief claim to fame, however, rests on its most notorious guest, William Hare, who lodged there on 6th February 1829 while on his way from Edinburgh to Portpatrick. With his partner Burke he had strangled a number of people and sold their bodies to anatomists for dissection. Burke was duly convicted and executed for these heinous crimes, but Hare escaped by turning King's evidence. After the trial he was to be deported to his native Ireland. News of his arrival in the burgh soon reached the ears of the multitude, and a vast mob gathered outside the hotel, hell-bent on executing summary justice on the body-snatcher. The Irish mail-coach was, with the greatest difficulty, permitted to leave the hotel yard after being minutely searched by the rabble. Meanwhile Hare was confined to his hotel room where, incredibly, the constabulary allowed many of the irate citizens' access. Hare was severely manhandled and almost strangled. As night fell the forces of law and order set up a decoy to distract the mob, while Hare was smuggled out of a rear window and secreted in the burgh jail for his own protection. The mob, cheated of their prey, laid siege to the jail and provoked a noisy riot that lasted for several hours. An attempt to burn the jail was repulsed by the burgh police who repeatedly baton-charged the rioters. The mob gradually evaporated and shortly before dawn, when the streets were deserted, he was spirited out of the jail by a sheriff's officer and two militiamen who escorted him on his way.

Dumfries in the 18th century had been a Tory stronghold, but after the retirement of David Staig in 1817 a more liberal attitude gradually prevailed. Dumfries escaped the repressive climate which affected many other towns in the years following Waterloo, and when Parliamentary Reform was mooted in 1830 the burgh greeted it enthusiastically. The Reform meeting held in the Court-house on 2nd December 1830 was the largest political gathering which had ever taken place in Dumfries up to that time. A second monster meeting on 15th March 1831 heartily approved the draft of the Reform Bill. The bill narrowly passed its second reading in the House of Commons on 21st March 1831, the member for the Dumfries Burghs (i.e. Annan, Lochmaben, Kirkcudbright and Sanquhar as well as Dumfries), William Douglas being among those who opposed the bill. At the General Election of May 1831, the delegates from Lochmaben, Sanquhar and Kirkcudbright favoured the sitting member, while Annan and Dumfries voted for the Reform candidate, General Sharpe of Hoddam. The delegates from 'the five Carlins' declared their choice at the Court house before a large crowd and Douglas was duly acclaimed the winner. It should be noted that the delegates who actually cast the votes were themselves chosen by their respective town councils - bodies which were still largely unrepresentative - so the entire process of electing MPs was undemocratic and prone to corruption. The ugly scenes that ensued threatened to repeat the mobbing of Hare two years earlier, and the re-elected member narrowly escaped serious injury. General Sharpe, on the other hand, was borne in triumph back to the King's Arms as if he had been the winner.

On 15th May 1832, the King's birthday, a mob gathered in the town and was incited by a radical demagogue whom the magistrates imprisoned as a result. The mob thereupon attacked the jail and threatened to burn it down; they were only dispersed with the greatest difficulty. Tempers ran high that summer as the Tories fought a fierce rearguard action in both Lords and Commons to frustrate the bill, but eventually it got its third reading and received the royal assent on 7th June. The number of Scottish MPs was increased from 45 to 53, but the most important result of the Reform Act was to replace the self-perpetuating old town councils by bodies which were elected by shopkeepers and householders possessing property valued at £10 per annum. This was still a very narrow franchise; the total number of 'ten pound voters' created in the five Dumfries burghs was only 967, of which 610 were in Dumfries itself. Not surprisingly, the Reform Act was celebrated by a civic gala held on 11th August 1832. At the next General Election, held later in December that year, General Sharpe was returned by a large majority. He retired in 1841 and was followed by William Ewart who held the seat till 1868. Thus was established the Whig, and latterly radical Liberal, dominance of Dumfries politics which was to continue till after the Second World War.

CHOLERA

The electoral triumph that marked the turning point in British politics was marred by the outbreak of the worst epidemic in centuries. Cholera, long endemic in India, reached Sunderland from Hamburg on 26th October 1831 in a bale of rags imported for the purpose of making paper. It erupted in a number of towns the following spring and the whole country was placed on the alert. A Board of Health was formed in Dumfries on 15th March 1832 and took measures to clean the slum tenements in the town centre and provide the inmates with nourishing soup. These steps came too little and too late. The town was insanitary and the Nith (from which the water supply was drawn) was polluted with sewage. Cholera reached Carlisle in July 1832 but the first victim in Dumfries, the widow Paterson of English Street, did not succumb till 16th September. For a week, victims died at the rate of one a day. The Rood Fair, held in the last week of September, was severely curtailed when the epidemic suddenly escalated. It peaked on 2nd October when there were 55 new cases and 44 deaths. Two days later there were 62 new cases but the mortality dropped to 27. Only eleven died the following day and from then onwards the epidemic gradually abated. A terrible thunderstorm on 4th October probably helped to clear the air. The disease continued its course till the middle of November, by which time there had been 837 cases in Dumfries and 421 deaths (187 males and 234 females). These were the official figures, but the sexton's accounts of the coffins required in that period show that the real number of deaths probably exceeded 550. In Maxwelltown there were 237 cases, of which 127 were fatal. Many of the victims were interred in a gigantic pit set aside at St Michael's for the purpose. The Cholera Mound lies on the west side of the churchyard and is surmounted by a monument whose lengthy inscription vividly recalls the catastrophe.

Water pump, dated 1804,
found in the basement of Mrs. McGowan's house.

The immediate outcome of the epidemic was a nationwide campaign for proper sanitation and improved water supply. In Dumfries itself various plans were proposed but came to nothing. The town continued with its unhygienic ways for almost twenty years. Then, on 16th November 1848, cholera struck again and between that date and the first week of January 1849 there were about 600 cases, of whom 317 died. Across the river there were 214 victims in Maxwelltown, of whom 114 succumbed. Goaded into action by this second visitation, the municipal authorities of the two burghs joined forces to promote a bill through Parliament. The Act of 10th May 1850 empowered a joint Water Commission whose members were partly elected by the two councils and partly by their respective ratepayers. The Commission instituted the waterworks which brought the precious liquid from Lochrutton four miles away on the principle of gravitation. Piped water did away with the time-honoured but insalubrious burn-drawers who perambulated the town with their wheeled barrels, selling water at the rate of five canfuls for a penny. 'There is now not a healthier town in the kingdom', commented a late-19th century gazetteer, but adding ominously, 'though there are yet several parts of the town that are disagreeable and unwholesome'. The introduction of the water supply was commemorated by a fountain erected on the Plainstones. This was replaced by the present ornamental cast-iron fountain in 1882.

£1 note of the Southern Bank of Scotland, 1839.

Parliamentary reform was soon followed by Burgh reform and a new Town Council was elected on the £10 franchise on 6th November 1833, Robert Murray becoming the first reform provost. An Act of 1846 abolished the privileges of burgh trade corporations. The Seven Incorporated Trades had been virtually defunct for several years. The few remaining members continued to hold the Trades property till March 1852 when the Siller Gun was consigned to the Town Council and the Trades Hall was sold for £650 to a merchant who converted it into business premises. The precious relics of the Trades, including the sword of the Red Comyn, the Grainger punch-bowl, the silverware and regalia, were disposed of on 8th April 1854, appropriately by public roup in the former Trades Hall, producing the relatively paltry sum of £54.

The General Police Act of 1834 led to the introduction of the rating system which defrayed the costs of policing, lighting, cleansing, paving and road-mending within the burgh. The first decennial Census was held in 1841, and it was then found that the population of Dumfries stood at 10,069. It rose steadily over the ensuing decades: 11,107 (1851), 12,313 (1861), 13,710 (1871), 15,759 (1881) and 16,675 (1891). By 1891 the burgh contained 3,863 occupied houses, 227 vacant houses and 21 under course of construction.

Prior to 1847 education in the burgh was largely the responsibility of the Academy. Freemen of the burgh were entitled to the free education of their children - a privilege which Burns claimed in respect of the freedom conferred on him in 1787 - but otherwise the school was fee-paying. The children of the poor received no education until 1847 when the Dumfries Ragged School was founded by David Stewart. Interestingly, the premises stood next door to Burns House. This provided schooling in the three Rs for the children of the destitute, but it also served as a reformatory for juvenile delinquents, the latter being boarded and lodged there. In time it was associated with a Common School where children of a somewhat higher class were educated free or for a nominal sum. The Education Act of 1870 made education compulsory and subsequently free and led to a tremendous expansion in the number and quality of schools both in Dumfries and across the river in Maxwelltown.

INTRODUCTION OF THE RAILWAY

The railway era came, so far as Dumfries was concerned, on 22nd August 1848 when a line was opened by the Caledonian Railway between the burgh and Gretna, where it connected with the main line from London via Carlisle to Glasgow. A direct line from Dumfries to Glasgow via Kilmarnock was opened as far as Closeburn on 15th October 1849. The Glasgow and South-Western Railway drove a line south of Kilmarnock to Auchinleck on 9th August 1848, extended to New Cumnock on 20th May 1850 and linked to Closeburn on 28th October the same year. A line from Dumfries westward was opened as far as Castle Douglas on 7th November 1859 by the Castle Douglas and Dumfries Railway Company which was absorbed by the G&SWR on 5th July 1865. The line from Castle Douglas to Stranraer was completed in March 1861 and extended to Portpatrick the following year. The last of the local railways was the Cairn Valley line which joined the main G&SWR line at Holywood in 1905. In the wake of the railways came the electric telegraph, originally designed to facilitate communications between railway stations and signal boxes. In May 1852 the Electric Telegraph Company opened its main Anglo-Irish line which fortunately lay through Dumfries and Galloway. The following year the G&SWR opened a telegraph from Dumfries to Glasgow following the route of its rail network. The British & Irish Magnetic Telegraph Company opened a rival system shortly afterwards. These private telegraph companies were nationalised in 1869 and responsibility for operating a unified system fell to the Post Office the following year.

The railway station was completely rebuilt in 1863 at what was then the north-eastern extremity of the town. It included a fine suite of offices, waiting rooms and a hotel. Until 1876 all of the railway buildings were on the west side of the tracks, but in 1875-6, preparatory to its becoming the working link between the Scottish systems and the English Midland system, new buildings, including a booking-hall, were erected on the east side and three times the previous accommodation for goods, together with sidings, engine-sheds and workshops. A spacious square for horse-wagons and carriages was laid out on the west side and the facilities were completed by the erection of a large railway hotel in 1896.

The co-founder of the American Navy, John Paul Jones, was born at Arbigland near Dumfries and his relatives had connections with the town. His niece Jane Young (Mrs David Williamson) inherited £700 from her uncle's estate and used this windfall to purchase the Commercial Hotel in the High Street, later renamed the County Hotel. Both it and the King's Arms were substantially renovated and expanded during the 19th century. Towards the close of the century the Queensberry Hotel, near the junction of English Street and the High Street and the George Hotel were erected. The Southern Counties Club was opened in Irish Street in 1874 and was noted for its huge billiard room.

Much of the town's prosperity in the second half of the 19th century rested on the textile industry. The vast Nithsdale woollen factory, a massive, turretted edifice that was quite palatial in aspect in its heyday, was built in 1858-9 and topped by a chimney stalk rising to a height of 174 feet. New mills were erected in Troqueer, Maxwelltown in 1866-7 and 1869-70 and to make it easier for the workforce to cross the river a third bridge was inaugurated on Hogmanay 1875. Costing almost £1,500, it was an iron suspension footbridge 203 feet in length. Kingholm Mills, where the Dumfries tweed industry originated, closed in 1893 and the plant and machinery were transferred to the Nithsdale and Troqueer Mills which had come under the same firm in 1871 and in their heyday gave employment to over 1,000 hands. Rosefield Woollen Mills, erected in 1887-9, had about 400 employees.

CHURCHES IN DUMFRIES

Dumfries shared in the extraordinary revival of organised religion which was one of the great hallmarks of Victorian Britain. By the 1890s Dumfries and Maxwelltown could boast more than a score of churches and chapels serving a wide variety of Christian denominations. St Michael's Church was completely rebuilt in 1744-5, given new pews in 1869 and entirely renovated in 1881. The original 'second church' was erected in 1727 on the site of Maxwell's Castle. It was demolished and rebuilt on a much larger scale to the design of the Edinburgh architect Starforth in 1866-7 at a cost of £7,000. Greyfriars Church, named in allusion to the monastery which had stood nearby in medieval times, was completed in 1868 by a spire 164 feet tall. A third Established Church, named St Mary's, was erected at the north end of English Street on the site of the medieval Chapel of Sir Christopher Seton in 1837-9 after designs by John Henderson of Edinburgh. It was renovated in 1878 and a hall, costing as much as the church itself, was added in 1888. Several churchmen of the district, notably the Rev. Dr Henry Duncan, played a prominent part in the Great Disruption of 1843 leading to the formation of the Free Church later that year. A Free church was built in George Street in 1843-44 at a cost of £1,400 and completely remodelled in 1893 at a cost of £2,000. The Martyrs' Free Church, formerly the Reformed Presbyterian Church, was built in Irving Street in 1831-2. The United Presbyterians had three churches; in Loreburn Street, Buccleuch Street and in Townhead Street. These churches, arising from the dissenting and seceding chapels of the 18th century, were rebuilt in 1829, 1862 and 1867 respectively. The Congregational Chapel in Irving Street was built in 1835, enlarged in 1862 and renovated in 1880. The Dumfries branch of the Evangelical Union was formed in 1862 and worshipped in the Assembly Rooms; plans to build a church in English Street never materialised and the sect gradually fizzled out, long before the Evangelists merged with the Congregationalists in 1896.

The English Church served the Episcopalians of Dumfries and the surrounding district who somehow survived the backlash of the Revolution. Several attempts were made by the Presbytery of Dumfries to stamp out 'Black Prelacy', but an Act of 1713 permitted Episcopal clergymen who took the oath abjuring the Jacobite cause to use the Anglican service in Scotland. Episcopal worship was conducted informally till 1756 when a chapel was erected in Lochmabengate. It was replaced by a handsome building on the corner of Buccleuch and Castle Streets in 1820, and this was sold to the Wesleyan Methodists in 1868 when St John's Church was erected in Newall Terrace in the First Pointed style, with a tower and spire 120 feet high. Farther along Newall Terrace, the Baptist Church (successor to a chapel in Irish Street) was opened in 1890.

The Catholic Church of St Andrew, pro-cathedral of the diocese of Whithorn or Galloway, was erected in 1811-13 in Shakespeare Street. Romanesque in style with Byzantine features, it received the addition of a fine tower (1843) and an octagonal spire (1858). Transepts and a domed apse were added in 1871-2 and the interior was beautifully decorated with arabesque ornament. These improvements were largely due to the generosity of the Maxwells of Terregles. St Andrew's was destroyed by fire in 1961, but subsequently rebuilt. The tower survived the conflagration and was retained as a memorial to the original church. Catholic schools for boys, girls and infants were located nearby. The original buildings having proved to be inadequate, a new Catholic boys' school was opened at Brooke Street in 1873 and placed under the charge of the Marist Brothers teaching order. Since 1874 the Marist Brothers have had their principal house at St Michael's Mount (formerly Laurel Bank) and it was here that Brother Walfrid, founder of Glasgow Celtic FC, laboured and died. A boarding school, St Joseph's College, was founded in 1875 on the site of the old burgh infirmary, but new and much larger premises were erected in the 1890s. A Catholic girls' school was opened in Brooke Street in 1896 and placed under the Sisters of Charity, a small community of which had been established in Dumfries in 1892. In 1884 a convent and church of the Benedictine Nuns were erected on Corbelly Hill and this includes a girls' boarding school. The various Catholic educational establishments in Dumfries owed an incalculable debt to the generosity of the Herries family.

What John and Charles Wesley were to England, James and Robert Haldane were to Scotland. These evangelists toured Scotland in the late 18th century and frequently visited Dumfries. In 1799 Robert Haldane, having been banned by the General Assembly from appearing in the pulpits of the Established Church, erected a spacious tabernacle or chapel in Buccleuch Street for the Independent congregation; but when the Hallidays defected to the Baptists the building had to be vacated. In 1814 the County Council purchased it and re-opened it two years later, totally refurbished, as a Court-house. When new County Buildings were opened in 1866, the Court-house was sold to the burgh for £1,020 and this became the Town Hall.

In 1883 the burgh jail was replaced by a new prison, serving the three southern counties and located on the western outskirts of Maxwelltown. The site of the old prison was acquired by the George Street Free Church. On part of the site they erected a large hall and then sold the rest of the ground to the Post Office for £1,125. Hitherto the post office serving Dumfries had been located in premises provided by the postmaster, a separate receiving office being sited in Maxwelltown. The accretion of the telegraph system (1870) and the establishment of the parcel post (1883), however, placed an intolerable burden on the post office then located in Queen Street. The town's first Crown office was opened in Buccleuch Street in May 1889. The Maxwelltown receiving office was then abolished, but another sub office was opened in St Michael's Street in November that year.

The birth centenary of Robert Burns was celebrated world-wide, but never more enthusiastically than in his adopted town where a banquet seating a thousand took place in the Nithsdale Mills, preceded by a vast procession through the streets. This celebration, however, was far exceeded in July 1896 by the commemorations surrounding the centenary of the poet's death. In 1882 a marble statue of Burns, sculpted by Amelia Hill, was unveiled opposite Greyfriars Church.

During the war scare of 1859, when it seemed that Napoleon III was intent on emulating his famous uncle, the militia (defunct since the Napoleonic War) was revived as the Galloway Rifles. Although the threat of war soon receded, the militia was kept in being and eventually became the 3rd Battalion, King's Own Scottish Borderers. Following the outbreak of the Anglo-Boer War in 1899 the 3rd KOSB served with distinction in South Africa and was feted by the town on its return in June 1902. William Robertson of Dumfries, a sergeant-major in the Gordon Highlanders, won the Victoria Cross and a battlefield commission for conspicuous gallantry at Elandslaagte. He received the freedom of the burgh on 24th December 1900.

THE TWENTIETH CENTURY

The years up to the outbreak of the First World War in 1914 saw relatively little change in the housing within the burgh. The last thatched houses were either demolished or re-roofed with slates in 1873. Handsome sandstone villas in Newall Terrace were erected in 1874-5 and similar dwellings of a superior quality, serving the rising middle classes of Dumfries, were built in Lovers' Walk, and along the Edinburgh, Moffat, Annan and Lockerbie Roads at the turn of the century. Similar expansion took place in Maxwelltown, in Laurieknowe and in the area bounded by Rotchell Road and the New Abbey Road. Little was done, however, to relieve the overcrowding and slum conditions in the inner town area until 1913 when a plan was evolved for the demolition of the decayed buildings in Munches Street (including cruck-framed houses) and the congested tenements to the east of Queensberry Square. This scheme, however, had to be partially shelved on account of the War. Nevertheless, Municipal Terrace was built the following year, at the junction of Brooms and Annan Roads, the first council housing erected anywhere in Scotland.

Dumfries retained its county market-town atmosphere. It never benefited from the full effects of the Industrial Revolution, but it was to escape the worst aspects of the post-industrial decline which many larger Scottish towns and cities were to suffer in the Sixties and Seventies. Such industry as Dumfries had tended to be centred on woollens and textiles; but at one point it seemed as if it might become Scotland's answer to Dagenham or Detroit. In the early years of this century the Drummond Motor Car Company launched the Serpent model (1909) and two years later the Arrol-Johnston Company established a large, modern car factory at Heathhall on the eastern outskirts of the town. During the War Arrol-Johnston switched to aircraft and armaments production.

Dumfries and Maxwelltown provided their share of men for the slaughter of the First World War, as the memorials in Newall Terrace and Rotchell Road testify. There were civic ceremonies to mark the departure of the 1/5 KOSB in August 1914, and the return of war veterans in 1919. The promise of homes fit for heroes was honoured in the 1920s when a number of ambitious housing schemes were undertaken. The first of these, at Janefield, consisted of 84 houses costing £80,000. Subsequently 144 houses were erected at Troqueer Holm at a total cost of £60,000 and 52 houses at Stonehousecroft cost only £20,000. These later but cheaper developments were just as good; the drastic cutting of costs merely reflected a much more efficient use of resources once building materials (subject to wartime controls) were deregulated. These schemes were but the start of a long line of housing projects which have completely transformed the character and appearance of the town.

The overcrowded slum area around Munches Street and Queensberry Square was eventually cleared in 1922-3 and the Wide Entry leading to Loreburn Street was replaced by a fine wide thoroughfare named Great King Street. There was considerable heartache when, in the course of clearing Queensberry Square and King Street, the Town Council sanctioned the removal of the domed gentlemen's convenience, popularly known as St Paul's. The slum dwellers were rehoused in the fine new schemes and the area was redeveloped for shops and offices. Among the splendid buildings which were erected in the 1920s in this area were the British Linen Bank, on the corner of Queensberry Square and Great King Street, and a new head post office farther up the street, inaugurated on 29th April 1926. On that date the former head post office in Buccleuch Street was closed. The new head post office and sorting office were greatly expanded in 1963. The re-organization of the Post Office in 1986, dividing it into Royal Mail Letters, Parcels and Counters, led to the downgrading of Dumfries which is now subordinate to Carlisle.

Many picturesque old buildings which might have been preserved, however, were allowed to decay and were then demolished. This was particularly regrettable in the Back Street (now Queensberry Street) where the Rainbow Stairs were demolished in 1934 making way for Burton's two years later. The Penthouse End, formerly the 'port' at the eastern end of the burgh, was demolished in 1931 but at least it was replaced by a building in the original style.

By the Twenties the so-called New Bridge of the 1790s, despite widening in 1893, was proving inadequate for the amount of motor traffic crossing the Nith. This congestion was relieved by the construction of the St Michael's Bridge (1927). Two years later, as the result of a plebiscite, the burghs of Dumfries and Maxwelltown were merged. This entailed a revision of the Dumfriesshire county boundary to take in a generous chunk of Kirkcudbrightshire. In the ensuing decade this permitted the development of even larger housing estates on the west bank of the Nith, at Troqueer, Sandside and the first phase of the Lincluden scheme, as well as extensive private development along Pleasance Avenue and the New Abbey Road. The last of the pre-war inner redevelopment took place in 1938 when old dwellings near Greyfriars Church were demolished to make way for the square and traffic roundabout. Burns's statue was resited as a result in the centre of the traffic flow.

The inter-war period was one of political and economic upheaval. Dumfries, in common with the rest of the country, was affected by the General Strike of 1926 but disturbances were minimal. Potentially a more serious threat came in the 1930s when the British Union of Fascists, led by Sir Oswald Mosley, gained a measure of credibility for a time and even Dumfries had its corps of Blackshirts. The Depression hit Dumfries hard. The Arrol-Johnston company, which constructed the famous Bluebird racing car in which Sir Donald Campbell gained the land speed record, was forced to merge with the Aster company in the late Twenties and went into liquidation in 1929. Hopes of re-opening the car factory were dashed by the economic climate of the following decade and the loss to the town was incalculable. Even the traditional mainstay of Dumfries was grievously affected and Charteris & Spence were forced to close their woollen mill, with considerable job losses. To some extent the worst effects of the Depression were offset by the massive programme of council housing and redevelopment that continued unabated.

The Second World War brought the Depression to an end. The old Arrol-Johnston factory was requisitioned by the RAF and an aerodrome was laid out on the nearby Tinwald Downs which had been a racecourse in Burns's time. In 1939 Imperial Chemical Industries opened an explosives plant at Drungans, west of Maxwelltown, and this was considerably expanded during the war.

In the late Forties Dumfries received a much-needed boost from light industry. The former car factory at Heathhall was taken over by the North British Rubber Company (later Uniroyal and now Gates Rubber Company). ICI expanded their wartime factory and diversified into plastics, with a fine new factory at Cargenbridge. Tweeds and knitwear continued to form the backbone of the local textile industry, but inevitably this suffered from competition from Southeast Asia and declined sharply in the 1960s and 1970s. No cloth is now manufactured in Dumfries, but knitwear factories continue to be operated by J. & D. McGeorge, Robertson and Wolsey. On the other hand, the position of Dumfries as the centre of an important agricultural area has been emphasised by the establishment of industries servicing agriculture, and the Carnation factory at Lincluden processes much of the milk produced in the region. The former wartime airfield at Tinwald Downs now forms one of several industrial estates in and around the town, providing a wide range of light-industrial enterprises.

Postwar development has been two-fold. A further accretion of land by Dumfries on the west bank of the Nith has been utilised for an industrial estate as well as the large housing schemes of Lincluden and Lochside. By 1962 Dumfries was officially clear of its last slums. Since 1900 the area of the burgh has risen five-fold but the population has only grown from 16,000 to its present level of 29,000. In the 1980s the main development, in both council schemes and private housing, took place on the east bank of the Nith, to the south of the town, notably in Calside and Georgetown while an extensive programme of modernising and upgrading the housing stock has taken place in more recent years.

Educational facilities have kept pace with the housing expansion. Dumfries Academy has trebled in size since the Second World War. Dumfries High School, formerly in George Street, was moved to spacious new premises in Marchmount, while a fine new Maxwelltown High School opened at Lincluden in 1970. The Dumfries High School premises in George Street served as a Technical College, prior to the establishment of the new buildings at Locharbriggs in the 1970s.

In 1906 twenty churches served eight denominations in Dumfries and Maxwelltown. Today there are 22 churches serving twelve denominations. The union of the Church of Scotland with the United Presbyterian and Free churches in 1900 and 1929 led to a rationalisation of the numerous sects that previously flourished, but in the course of this century there has been an expansion in the religious coverage of the town. Not all of the free churches acceded to the union and to this day the Free Church and the United Free Church are represented. But, in addition, there are now churches serving the Christian Brethren, Jehovah's Witnesses, Salvation Army, Spiritualists, Christian Scientists, Society of Friends and the Latter Day Saints (Mormons). In 1989 there was a proposal to convert the old Loreburn Street Church into a mosque serving the town's growing Moslem population, but this plan was blocked and instead the church was acquired as an extension to the Ewart Library. Several other churches in the inner urban area were closed or relocated in the new housing estates, reflecting the shift of population.

Cresswell Maternity Hospital was one of the more tangible benefits to arise from the National Health scheme introduced at the end of the Second World War. An enormous new Royal Infirmary, costing over £4 millions, was inaugurated by Queen Elizabeth on a spacious site off Bankend Road in 1975.

In matters of transport, however, the present century has witnessed savage retrenchment. Motor buses made their debut in 1921 and, together with the rise in private ownership of motor cars, made passenger trains uneconomic. The last line to be developed, the Cairn Valley Light Railway of 1905, was the first to go. Pasenger services ceased on 3rd May 1943 and freight traffic six years later. The branch line from Dumfries to Lockerbie closed to pasengers on 19th May 1952 and to goods on 4th May 1964. The biggest blow of all, however, came on 14th June 1965 when the Galloway line from Dumfries to Stranraer via Castle Douglas and Newton Stewart was abolished. Henceforward rail travellers from Dumfries to Stranraer were faced with a much longer journey via Kilmarnock, Ayr and Girvan, and even this route was threatened with closure in 1990. The old Glasgow and South-Western route through Kirkconnel, Dumfries and Annan to Carlisle is now a shadow of its former self, with far fewer trains since 1970 and no through services to London any longer.

The re-organization of local government in Scotland in 1974 has had sweeping repercussions. The three southwestern counties now form Dumfries and Galloway Region, and the former County Buildings have since been expanded out of all recognition to accommodate the regional services. The burgh has been absorbed in Nithsdale District and the Town Hall on Buccleuch Street is now its headquarters. One of the last plans devised before regionalisation was a new bridge across the Nith near the Academy, leading to an inner ring road along Lovers' Walk. This scheme, roundly condemned both locally and nationally, was mercifully scrapped. Fifteen years later the long looked for Dumfries By-pass is about to reach fruition, with a bridge spanning the Nith near its confluence with the Cluden Water. This will divert most of the traffic between Ireland and the Continent from its present course (either across St Michael's Bridge or along Loreburn Street) and then Dumfries will revert to a tranquillity which it has not experienced since the 19th century.

There was a further surge of redevelopment in Dumfries in the late 1970s and throughout the 1980s, arresting that inner urban decay which had befallen many towns and cities in the post-industrial period. This has been most noteworthy in the Southergate, where a large Presto (now Safeway) supermarket was erected in 1980 and where (across the street) a shopping mall is planned for 1990. For some years it was feared that such a shopping facility would be established outside the town, after the manner of such developments in North America. Such a mall would have hit the shopping facilities in the town centre very hard. In the same period the High Street has been transformed, as national chain stores such as Marks & Spencer, Argos, Next and Littlewood's have appeared on the local scene. It is a matter for considerable regret that the arrival of Marks & Spencer meant the loss of the old County Hotel, one of the town's best-loved historic landmarks, while the even more venerable King's Arms was demolished to make way for Boot's and Mothercare. At the time of writing, however, the wheel appears to have come full circle. In 1989 the High Street was pedestrianised, and this process was extended to the open spaces at either end. Not everyone agrees with the changes which have been wrought around the Burns statue, but motor traffic is now confined to Buccleuch and Academy Streets. At the other end, Queensberry Square was scheduled for completion in mid-1990, the last phase being a new shopping complex on the north side. The former Trades Hall was substantially refurbished and restored in the late 1980s; while externally it looks much as it did in 1804, it is now a Burger King fast-food restaurant, symbolic of the times we live in.

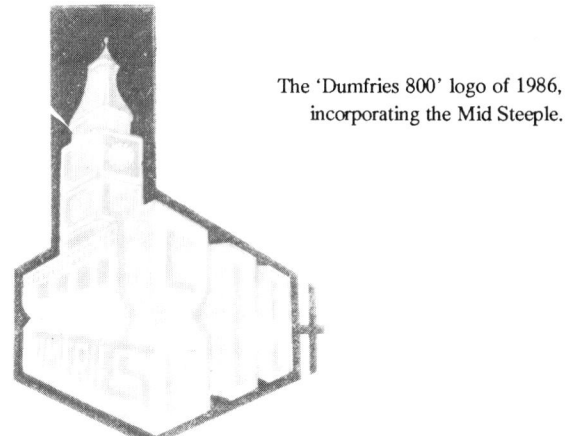

The 'Dumfries 800' logo of 1986, incorporating the Mid Steeple.

Despite all the vicissitudes and upheavals, especially within the last hundred years, Dumfries continues to go from strength to strength. In 1986 year-long celebrations marked the Octocentenary of the burgh chartered by King William the Lion, and now, in the 1990s, plans are being laid for the fitting commemoration of the Bicentenary of the death of Robert Burns who, more than any man before or since, put Dumfries on the world map.

DUMFRIES, VIEWED FROM THE NEW BRIDGE, 1840 — This engraving shows the foreshore of the Whitesands on the left. Devorgilla's Old Bridge, which dates from the 14th century, dominates the background. Most of the buildings in this picture are still standing, 150 years later. The steeple of St Michael's (far left) and the observatory tower of the Museum (right background) are prominent landmarks to this day.

QUEENSBERRY SQUARE, 1840 — In the foreground is the High Street, looking south towards the Mid Steeple (erected 1707) and the Trades Hall (erected 1804). The Queensberry memorial pillar (left) is to be restored to its original location after an absence of 56 years.

THE BURNS MAUSOLEUM — The mortal remains of Scotland's National Bard were originally interred in an unmarked grave but in 1813 plans were set in motion for the erection of a Mausoleum. Plans by Thomas Hunt were approved in 1815 and on 5th June that year the foundation stone was laid. The poet's remains were transferred to the Mausoleum on 19th September 1817, together with the coffins of his children Francis Wallace (1789–1803) and Maxwell (1796–99). The vault was opened on 1st April 1834 for the burial of the poet's widow Jean Armour and last disturbed in May 1857 when Burns's eldest son, Robert Junior, was laid to rest. This the earliest photograph of the Mausoleum (1850) records the visit of Thomas Aird and two of the poet's sons, Colonel William Nicol Burns and Robert Burns Junior.

THE GALLOWAY RIFLE VOLUNTEERS— The earliest references to the raising of local military forces in Dumfries date from the 1670s. Trained bands had, of course, rallied to the defence of the town and surrounding district since the Border wars with England in the 13th and 14th centuries. Later, men responded to the call to arms to defend the town during the Jacobite rebellions of 1715 and 1745-6. The Royal Dumfries Volunteers, which numbered Robert Burns in their ranks, were raised in 1795 for the defence of the realm. Militia units were disbanded at the end of the Napoleonic Wars (1815) but when 'Haughty Gaul invasion threatened' in 1858 the militia movement was resurrected. The Galloway Rifle Volunteers were formed on that occasion. Their cap badge (right) was the Lion Rampant in a thistle wreath, surmounted by the Victorian crown and GRV.

FIRMS' BILL–HEADS — Many of the shopkeepers in Dumfries decorated their bill–heads and stationery with engravings that showed their premises. Andrew Patterson's clothier shop was located at 76 High Street opposite the Fountain which appears prominently in this charming vignette (above). James Swan—'Linen & Woollen Draper, Silk Mercer, Hosier &c'—used several different engravings that subtly updated the displays in his windows at 54–55 High Street (below).

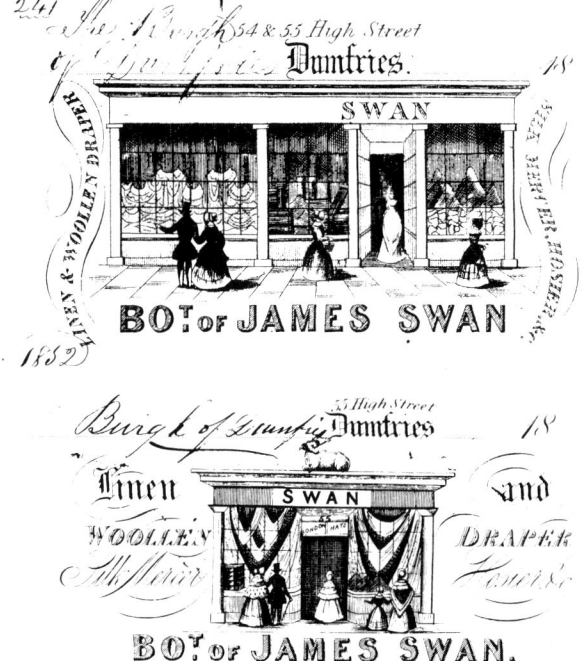

ROBERT BELL'S IRONMONGERY SHOP, HIGH STREET — This photograph, taken in the late 1850s, is one of the earliest of a Dumfries street scene. Robert Bell (wearing a top hat and standing to the right of the shop doorway) was one of the leading townsmen of his day. Binns department store later occupied the site of this ironmongery shop. In the foreground is a horse cab at the Long Range stance near the Fountain.

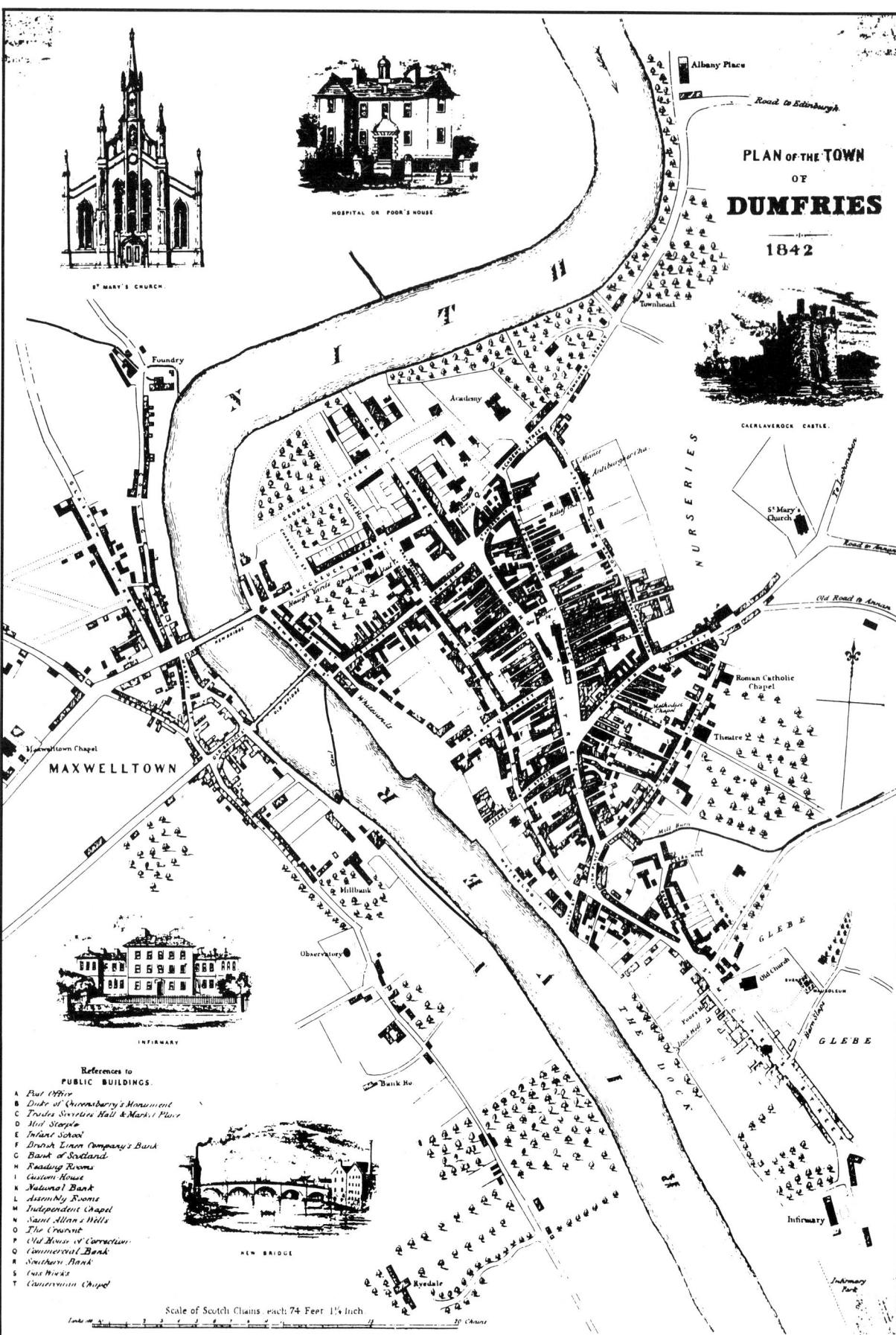

THE BURGH OBSERVATORY — from a *carte de visite*, 1860. This building began life in the 18th century as a windmill and, situated on Corbelly Hill in Troqueer parish, was one of the most prominent landmarks of the district. The mill fell into disuse in 1834 but was rescued from destruction and transformed into an Observatory the following November. This enterprise was funded by a share issue and shareholders were given metal 'tickets' in the form of medals struck in Birmingham, with a view of the tower on the obverse and their name and number engraved on the reverse. A museum was added and, under the administration of Nithsdale District Council, is now one of the town's most popular attractions, together with a camera obscura affording panoramic views of the town and surrounding district.

QUEENSBERRY SQUARE LOOKING EAST — This photograph, about 1860, was taken from the Mid Steeple. The only building which has survived to this day is the Trades Hall (extreme right). Sold off in 1847 for £650, it became successively business premises and shops, the show-rooms and offices of the Electricity Board and is now a restaurant. The buildings in the background were demolished in the 1920s to make way for the British Linen Bank and Great King's Street. The Square was laid out in 1770, following the destruction of the New Wark. The Doric pillar in the centre was erected in memory of Charles, Duke of Queensberry (died 1778) in recognition of his many benefactions to the burgh.

GREYFRIARS CHURCH UNDER CONSTRUCTION — The so-called New Kirk was erected in 1727 but 140 years later had fallen into such a ruinous state as to be a hazard to its congregation as well as passers-by. It was demolished in 1865 and replaced soon afterwards by a new church. Controversy raged over the choice of Greyfriars as the name of the new building, alluding to the medieval monastery which had existed nearby. During the demolition and excavation of the foundations many relics of the old castle of Dumfries came to light. The foundation stone of Greyfriars was laid on 11th May 1866 and the imposing structure, designed by the Edinburgh architect Starforth, was erected in 1867–68. The photograph shows the rather primitive scaffolding required during the construction of the steeple. The New Medical Hall, at the entrance to Castle Street on the left, was demolished in 1938 when Greyfriars Place was widened to make a traffic roundabout.

THE ACADEMY IN 1870 — Built at the beginning of the 19th century, the Academy was completely redeveloped in the 1890s. Among the boys playing cricket in the foreground is the young James Maxwell Barrie (author of Peter Pan), born in Kirriemuir but educated in Dumfries.

ALEXANDER'S CARPENTRY YARD, 1872 — Mr Alexander conducted his carpentry business at Bowhouses near Terregles (now on the western outskirts of Dumfries). To judge by the wooden articles in various stages of completion littered around the yard, Mr Alexander manufactured everything from wagons and carts to barrels and tubs and thus combined with carpentry the crafts of the cooper and the wheelwright.

CARPENTER'S YARD, c1910 — The above photograph is of Frank Preacher's carpentry yard in Howgate Street Dumfries.

DUMFRIES STRATHSPEY BAND, 1880 — A tradition for fiddle music was well established in Dumfries, long before the visit of the celebrated Neil Gow in the 1790s. This photograph portrays James and Thomas Bell (Kirkmahoe), Thomas Edgar (Glenhowan), Ed Smith (Netherholm), Mr Rintoul (Factor to Leny of Dalswinton), Mr Tibbets (Collector of Water Rates), Maxwell Wright (Benerick), Mr Crockett (Terregles) and Mr Tait (Lochrutton). Mr McKettrick (banker) was also a member but is not shown in this picture.

THREE CROWNS CLOSE — This was one of the long narrow closes which linked Loreburn Street and Queensberry Street and which were demolished shortly before the First World War in the first phase of slum clearance in the inner town area. The close derived its name from the Three Crowns Hotel. The cobblestones have, however, survived to this day.

HORSE AND CATTLE MARKET, WHITESANDS — From the earliest times a cattle fair was held on the Whitesands every Monday, but in 1659 this was changed to Wednesdays to avoid desecration of the Sabbath. Two horse fairs were held annually, at Candlemas (February) and in September, the latter being known as the Rood Fair and confirmed by a charter granted by James VI in 1621. By the late 19th century over 30,000 cattle, mainly from Galloway, were sold annually at Dumfries.

DUMFRIES FROM THE SOUTH — This is the caption on a photograph taken about 1880 by John Valentine of Dundee, but it would be more accurate to describe it as a view of the town taken from the west bank of the Nith. Running diagonally across the foreground is the Caul, the weir which controlled the flow of the river. Below the Caul, the Nith is tidal. Note the four carriages parked along the railings; the site is now a busy car park. The buildings at the rear of the Whitesands have remained much as they were a century ago.

LOREBURN ST JOHN'S SCHOOL — This primary school served the population in the congested district around Queensberry Square and Loreburn Street The brighter pupils might win a scholarship to the Academy if they were lucky—and if their parents could afford to keep them on at school; but most pupils left at the age of twelve for domestic service or labouring jobs. The little girls in this photograph of 1881 are all well turned out with a preponderance of pinafores, a practical bibbed apron which protected the dress.

GEORGETOWN SUNDAY SCHOOL OUTING — Robert Raikes founded the Sunday School movement in the 1780s to provide a grounding in the three Rs for the children of the poor who would not otherwise get any education. A century later, free and compulsory education was guaranteed at primary level and the aim of Sunday schools was almost entirely religious. Today Georgetown is a vast housing estate but in the 1890s it was truly rural, the children walking a mile and a half to Gasstown to attend primary school and church.

DUMFRIES OTTER HOUNDS, 1885 — Adult outings more than a century ago were rather grimmer in character and otter-hunting was a popular pursuit in an age when nature conservation was virtually unheard of. The long poles were for prodding river banks to dislodge the otters.

SMITHY IN A CLOSE OFF THE HIGH STREET — The horse continued to be the chief means of transport in and around Dumfries until the First World War. While France, Germany and the United States were forging ahead with horseless carriages Britain was hampered by reactionary legislation which effectively kept the motor vehicle at bay until 1904. Traces of mews and stables abound in the town to this day, but the smithies and coach-repairers in the cobbled closes off the High Street are long gone.

LORD ROSEBERY AT THE TOWN HALL — The Earl of Rosebery, arguably the most prominent Burnsian of his day as well as a leading Liberal politician who eventually became Prime Minister (1894–95), was the principal orator on two Burns occasions in Dumfries. In 1882 he unveiled the statue of the poet and fourteen years later he presided over the commemoration marking the centenary of the poet's death. This picture shows the Earl arriving in an open carriage at the Town Hall, its portico suitably garlanded for the occasion.

THE BURNS STATUE — Following the erection of the Burns statue in George Square, Glasgow in 1872 a campaign for a similar edifice in Dumfries got under way, but it was not until 1877 that the project was practically launched. £500 was raised within a year, but the crash of the City of Glasgow Bank in 1878 hindered progress. A grand exhibition of Burns relics and bazaar in 1880 raised a similar sum and, together with substantial donations, enabled the statue committee to bring the project to fruition. A figure of Burns modelled by Amelia Hill was selected and a life-sized statue was subsequently carved in Carrara marble. The statue was unveiled on 6th April 1882.

THE BURNS STATUE, c.1900 — The statue, one of the best-known landmarks in Dumfries, has moved its location four times, mainly due to road-widening and the re-arrangement of the traffic. This photograph shows the original location near the entrance to Castle Street. The railings were removed during the Second World War.

CASTLE STREET, 1938 — The buildings in the picture above were demolished in 1938 to permit road widening in Greyfriars Place. The Burns Statue was then re-sited in the centre of a traffic roundabout. In 1990 the High Street was pedestrianised and the statue enclosed within a low walled garden.

BUCCLEUCH STREET — Named after the Duke of Queensberry and Buccleuch, it was laid out in the 1790s after the opening of the New Bridge and ran eastward to the northern end of the High Street and the New Church (now Greyfriars) which can be seen in the background. This photograph dates from 1893 when the bridge was substantially widened and, apart from the cobblestones, it remains virtually unaltered to this day.

COUNTY COURT HOUSE, BUCCLEUCH STREET — One of the noblest architectural achievements of the town, the Court House was completed in time for the Spring Assizes of April 1866. Constructed in the Scottish Baronial style from a design by David Rhind, its tall peaked towers and open Italianate parapets gave it immediately the characteristics of a castle and the softer lines of a palace. Its relatively low-lying site, however, robbed it of that eminence which its design and purpose deserved. Alongside, and dwarfed by it, was the head post office (opened in 1889) and beyond, the United Presbyterian Church (erected in 1863).

TINKERS AT THE WHITESANDS — The covered wagons of itinerant workers, gipsies and tinkers were a familiar sight at the turn of the century and the wide area along the Whitesands provided a convenient campsite in the very heart of the town. The wagons are shown here approximately where the Tourist Information Office now stands.

TINKERS BY THE OLD BRIDGE — This photograph of about 1895 shows a tinker encampment on the Whitesands beside the Old Bridge re-built in the mid-15th century on the site of the bridge originally constructed by order of the Lady Devorgilla. The bridge lost one of its arches in 1794 when the roadway was widened in the approach to the New Bridge, while another arch was removed in 1825. This necessitated the insertion of the flight of steps which put an end to vehicular traffic on the Old Bridge.

TINKERS' CAMP–FIRE — The tinkers made their camp under the most primitive conditions, and cooked over open fires whose glow was one of the evening attractions for the citizens taking a stroll along the Whitesands. The caravans in the background are little more than carts with tarpaulins thrown over hoops—a far cry from the elaborate gipsy wagons with their brightly painted wooden roofs, usually associated with travelling people.

JEAN BRAND AND BIDDIE — Jean Brand was a blind fiddler who made a precarious living as a strolling player, invariably guided by her barefoot companion known simply as Biddie. In this picture they are wearing alpaca 'coal–scuttle' bonnets over white linen mutches, and Irish plaid cloaks which conceal voluminous petticoats.

THE GLENCAPLE HORSE-BUS — Open charabancs drawn by pairs of horses provided a frequent service between Dumfries and Glencaple. These services were operated by rival families, the Clarks and the Fishers, whose cut-throat competitiveness assumed the proportions of a vendetta at times, with drivers cracking their whips across the heads of the passengers seated on the coach of their rival and occasionally descending to fisticuffs in the roadway. The horse-bus is here shown outside its Dumfries terminus, the Commercial Hotel in the High Street.

THE ROOD FAIR — By 1895 when this photograph was taken, the Rood Fair had ceased to be the great agricultural market of bygone times and had become instead the town's most important annual holiday, dominated by a fairground with carousels and sideshows. The people of Dumfries and the surrounding district flocked to the Whitesands.

THE ACADEMY — The nucleus of the Academy existed as long ago as 1481 when Robert Turnbull was described in a sasine as rector of the school of 'Drumfries'. Robert Burns secured free education for his sons at the grammar school in the 1790s by virtue of the freedom of the burgh conferred on him in 1787. Extensive additions were made to the original building in 1871 and in the following year it was placed under the management of a School Board which instituted an entirely new building. Designed by Frank Carruthers this building, which was opened in September 1897 at a cost of £16,000, still stands.

ACADEMY CLASSROOM, c 1910 — This photograph was reproduced from the J. Rutherford collection which forms a part of the archives of the Crichton Museum. Mr Rutherford, born at New Farm, left home at the age of fifteen and started a drapers business in Bristol. The business was so successful he was able to retire after a period of about sixteen years. On his retiral he returned to Dumfries and bought the small estate of Jardington on the banks of the Cluden. He was renowned as an expert photographer and an authority on many scientific matters.

MARKET SQUARE AND PLAINSTANES — This was the very heart of the old burgh, showing the western side of the High Street running back to Greyfriars Church. The Mid Steeple (erected 1707) is the prominent landmark in the background and on the right is the building which, in the 17th and 18th centuries, contained the Council Chamber, coffee house and newspaper room. In the 19th century this became Ingram's Coffee House Hotel and later the licensed premises of John Raphael. These buildings were demolished in 1934 to make way for Burton's tailoring establishment. In the foreground stands the ornamental Fountain, itself dating from December 1882 and replacing an earlier and much plainer one commemorating the installation of piped water in 1851. The railings were removed as part of the salvage drive during the Second World War.

STREET MARKET, PLAINSTANES — Since time immemorial the cobbled area south of the Mid Steeple was used for the sale of fruit and vegetables by the smallholders and market gardeners of the district. Displayed on trestle tables are the cabbages offered by 'Chaiwie' Kennedy (in straw boater). Note the barefoot urchins (left), otherwise quite formally dressed. In the background stand the premises of James Maxwell (founded 1846), stationers and booksellers which were later taken over by Robert Dinwiddie.

THE INFIRMARY — A new hospital, together with its site, was acquired by Dumfries as the result of a generous donation of £5,000 from Mrs Laurie of Maxwelton, matched by a similar sum raised by public subscription. The total cost amounted to about £12,000. The Infirmary was designed by John Starforth and the foundation stone laid on 16th September 1869. The statuary adorning the doorway was sculpted by John Currie. £3,000 was raised from the public at the time of Queen Victoria's Diamond Jubilee (1897) and the money used for the provision of a nurses' home and a TB sanatorium opened in July 1900. On the Infirmary being relocated south of the town in 1975 the old building was renamed the Nithbank Hospital and is now used mainly for administrative purposes.

DAVID McMILLAN — This shop was located at 29 Friars Vennel and purveyed a wide range of goods and services. Basically a newsagent and tobacconist, McMillan was also a printer, stationer and fishing tacklemaker as his signboard signifies. He seems to have been an optician of sorts, to judge by the window notice advertising spectacles for sale. The newsboard on the right, referring to Joseph Chamberlain and Radium, dates this photograph to the early 1900s.

WEST END OF THE HIGH STREET — Superficially the High Street west of the Mid Steeple has hardly changed in the past century. The cobblestones were later tarmaced but in the process of pedestrianisation completed in 1990 have reverted to paving stones once more. The gas lamps were replaced by electric lighting in 1911. Many of the shops remain although the businesses occupying them have changed. Young's umbrella shop, on the corner of Friars Vennel (extreme right), celebrated its centenary in 1970 and survived a further decade, but has now been superseded by a Building Society — a trend that is nationwide.

QUEENSBERRY SQUARE — The loafers who congregated around the Queensberry pillar were jocularly known as the Monument Rangers. The domed public lavatory with its elaborate ironwork cupola was nicknamed St Paul's. The building on the left, occupied by the clothier N. McKie and J. Cleworth's grocery shop, later became the Dumfries & Maxwelltown Co-operative Society and now (1990) is being elegantly refurbished.

THE THEATRE ROYAL — Now the oldest provincial theatre still active in Scotland, it was first opened in 1792. The original subscribers had silver tickets entitling them to free admission. Robert Burns took an active part in its foundation, secured the services of Alexander Nasmyth as a scene painter, and wrote prologues for actresses. He had ambitions to become a playwright but died before they could be realised. The Theatre was designed by Thomas Boyd, after the Theatre Royal in Bristol, and originally (as shown in this photograph of 1900) had the royal arms at the front of the roof. In 1909 it became a cinema, known as the Electric Theatre (or popularly as 'The Auld Scratch' on account of its reputation as the proverbial flea–pit). The legitimate stage was not forgotten and repertory groups played several seasons before the Second World War. The wheel came full circle when the cinema closed and was acquired by the Guild of Players who have restored it to its original role.

THE ELECTRIC THEATRE — It seems remarkable that Dumfries, as late as 1951 when this picture was taken (bottom right), boasted three cinemas—the Lyceum, the Playhouse and the Electric Theatre. A survey of habits carried out by Glasgow University that year commented 'There is little evidence that Dumfries is greatly addicted to cinema–going. Nearly 47 per cent of our sample attend only once a month or less frequently; and that, by any contemporary standards, can hardly be regarded as excessive.' Television came a few years later and only the Lyceum (now the Cannon, in Shakespeare Street) survived the competition. The Electric Theatre closed its doors but, as already noted, eventually re–emerged once more as the Theatre Royal. In this photograph can be seen the spire of St Andrew's Cathedral. In the foreground is Miss Constantine's sweetie shop.

LAYING THE FOUNDATION STONE OF THE EWART LIBRARY — In 1898 Provost Glover approached Andrew Carnegie regarding help in establishing a new library. Carnegie provided £10,000 and the site was gifted by Mr Thomas McKie and Miss McKie of Moat House. The plans were drawn up by Alan Crombie and the foundation stone laid on 13th October 1899 by Miss McKie. The ceremony closed with the presentation of the freedom of the burgh to Carnegie on whose suggestion the building was named in honour of the late William Ewart, long-time MP for the Dumfries Burghs and architect of the Free Libraries Act.

WELCOME HOME — On the outbreak of the second Anglo-Boer War in October 1899 the Dumfries and Galloway Rifle Volunteers both sent contingents for active service in South Africa. The militia, now the 3rd Battalion KOSB, was called up for garrison duties early in 1900 but volunteered for active service and was despatched to the Cape in April that year. On its return in June 1902 the regiment was feted and the freedom of the burgh conferred on its field officers. Provost Glover is shown greeting the troops from the steps of the Mid Steeple. The Grecian portico at the top of the steps was removed in 1907. The Mid Steeple was then occupied by J. Hiddleston, clothier and draper but today houses the District Registrar's offices.

OPENING THE EWART LIBRARY (above) — The building was completed in 1904. The opening ceremony was performed by Miss McKie and on this occasion both Andrew Carnegie and two daughters of William Ewart were present.

WILLIAM GORDON'S TOBACCO STORE — This shop in the High Street next door to the County Hotel was, as the sign denotes, established in 1745, the original proprietor being Robert Mundell. His daughter married Provost Gabriel Richardson and became the mother of Sir John Richardson, the Arctic explorer. A son was James Mundell, the surgeon who became a close friend of Robert Burns and with him was lampooned by the right-wing Loyal Natives. The carved and painted wooden figure above the doorway was a characteristic sign of a tobacconist's shop, though Red Indians and Highlanders were more usually employed for this purpose.

CURLING ON THE NITH — During the winter of 1902 the temperature plummetted to a record low. The devotees of the roaring game were quick to take advantage of this and an impromptu rink was established near the New Bridge, providing an unusual view of the match to spectators on the footpath overhead.

NUNHOLM LADIES' HOCKEY TEAM — The squad for the season of 1903–04 are shown here, resplendent in their fur–trimmed tam o' shanters, sashes and serge ankle–length skirts with white trim.

KOSB AT HANNAHFIELD — In 1875 the estate of Hannahfield, including Kingholm Merse, was conveyed by deed of gift from the Crown to the War Department, with power to use it as a place of encampment and a parade ground for the local militia during annual training. The estate had originally belonged to John Hannah whose nephew's widow, having died intestate, resulted in the lands reverting to the Crown in 1869. The picture shows the Hannahfield hutments in the background and temporary marquees at the side. Shown above are officers of the 3rd KOSB, under the command of Lieutenant-Colonel James Maxwell-Witham, CMG.

DUMFRIES CRICKET CLUB — The photograph shows the bachelors composing the Single Team who took on the married members on 8th September 1906. Back row (left to right): N. Sloan, R. Sloan, G.I. Hendrie, S. Hutchison, S. Dickie, A. Douglas. Front row: P. Hepworth, W.S. Johnston, A. Jardine, A.C. Craig, A.F. Black and W.S. Millar.

ONE OF THE FIRST CARS IN DUMFRIES — This open touring horseless carriage of March 1903 was constructed at Lanark by J.C. Stirling to the design of Commandant Krebs, a director of the French Panhard company. At the wheel is James Alexander Butler with Peter Wilson as passenger. Butler was then an 18 year-old apprentice with Drummond's. Four years later he went out to Assam as an engineer.

SANTA CLAUS AT THE WHEEL, 1905 — The gaily bedecked car is an Argyll, with the licence number SM 100. It is shown here in the yard of W. Irving, coach- and car-hirers, whose premises were located at the rear of the King's Arms Hotel.

DUMFRIES BOAT CLUB — A rowing club, with its boat–house, was established on the east bank of the Nith in the 1850s. This photograph shows club members at the beginning of this century.

DRAMA AT THE THEATRE ROYAL — This scene from 'Hook and Eye' shows Miss McDowall as Sylvia Selbourne, W.A. Aitken as Joshua Gelding, A.F. Black as Harry Selbourne and J. Kissock as Edward Farleigh.

ROSEFIELD MILLS — In 1885 Samuel Charteris and Robert Spence purchased the property of Rosefield next door to the Troqueer Mills and erected the Rosefield Mills, designed by Alan Crombie. This factory, the most advanced in its day, had a frontage on the Nith of 130 metres, with electric light and the most modern power looms. The west view of the Rosefield Mills, seen from across the river, was one of the most impressive sights in the town. In the 1980s, however, production ceased, the mills were demolished and the site has since been redeveloped for housing. The vignettes are taken from a Charteris & Spence trade card of about 1906.

TROQUEER MILLS — The textile industry was the largest employer of labour at the turn of the century, with about 1500 hands in the mills on both banks of the Nith. The success of this enterprise was due largely to the Scott family. In 1846 Robert Scott acquired a sawmill at Kingholm and converted it into a mill for spinning hosiery yarn. Soon afterwards the firm diversified into tweeds. Scott retired in 1851 and his sons expanded the business. Walter Scott dissolved the partnership with his brother John in 1866 and moved across the Nith, establishing the Troqueer Mills in Maxwelltown. By 1871 this establishment had 532 hands and 10,780 spindles. Walter Scott passed on the mills to his sons Charles and Henry in 1885. The Nithsdale Mills were sold in 1902, but the Troqueer Mills remained in the hands of the Scott family. The photograph shows the staff of the Designing Office and Pattern Shop in August 1905.

WILLIAM RICHARDSON, 1908 — The well-known monumental mason and builder is portrayed here with his Pomeranian dogs and strawberry barrels in his garden adjoining the builder's yard which was situated at the corner of Glebe Street and Hood's Loaning (where Wyllie's grain store now stands). The steeple of St Michael's is visible in the background. The child in cloth cap and large lace collar was Richardson's granddaughter (later Mrs Aitken).

THE DOCK PARK BANDSTAND — The stretch of open ground from the Caul to Castledykes was known as the Dock from the quay occupying the waterfront, but usage declined sharply after the coming of the railways in the 1850s. In Burns's time it was used as a parade ground by the Royal Dumfries Volunteers, and this era is recalled by the carronades of the Napoleonic War. Early in the 19th century cast-iron benches were provided for the deserving poor and the park, with its many recreational facilities, is now maintained by Nithsdale Council. The bandstand was inaugurated, amid a large concourse, in 1906.

THE RISE ON THE NITH (above) — This three-masted schooner, registered at Marstal in Denmark, is said to have been the last sailing ship to navigate the Nith entirely under wind power. She is shown here sailing downstream on 30th March 1924. Since then shipping on the river has been largely confined to pleasure craft which use the tiny harbour at Kingholm.

THE GENERAL HAVELOCK AT THE NEW DOCK, 1907 (right) — This two-masted schooner of 40 tons register was built at Conway, North Wales in 1858 for the Solway coastal trade. At the time of the photograph she belonged to J. Wright & Company, wholesale grocers of Dumfries who used her to bring bulk goods by sea right into the heart of the town and unloading at the New Dock, Castledykes. Later she belonged to J. Kingan & Sons of New Abbey who used the Bog Quay there to bring in timber for their business and taking out farm produce. Mr Cannon of Carsethorn was her last skipper. By the mid 1920s her masts had been cut back and she was fitted with a 25 HP Kelvin auxiliary engine. She was sold, in sailing order, at Annan in 1937 for £5 and subsequently broken up for firewood.

THE FUNERAL OF EX-PROVOST GLOVER — Joseph Johnstone Glover demitted the office of Provost in 1905 after a period of nine years. Arguably the most influential and able of the civic leaders since the time of David Staig, he was widely mourned at the time of his death in April 1908. The photograph shows his funeral cortege proceeding up Buccleuch Street. Horse-drawn hearses continued to be used in Dumfries till the 1930s.

THE HIGH STREET AND MID STEEPLE — This postcard, dating from the end of the Edwardian era, shows handcarts and horse-drawn vehicles but no motor cars. By now the Coffee House Hotel was in the hands of Hugh Logan who was proprietor from 1894 till 1902.

ACADEMY AMATEUR DRAMATICS — The Academy has a long tradition of amateur theatrical productions of a very high quality. Many members of the Guild of Players first trod the boards at the Academy. The comic operas of Gilbert and Sullivan were perennial favourites, especially 'The Pirates of Penzance' which was staged on several occasions.

DANCING BEAR. Itinerants known as Ursari travelled all over Europe for centuries, entertaining bystanders with their dancing bears. A toot on a bugle brought people out on to the street to witness the impressive spectacle of a Brown Bear (standing up to eight feet tall) lumbering rhythmically on the cobblestones. The youthful audience is mainly barefoot — from choice rather than necessity. The Hole i' the Wa' in the background still stands in the High Street and is alleged to have had associations with Robert Burns.

THE CONVENT SCHOOL, c.1910 — The Convent of the Benedictine Order of Nuns of the Perpetual Adoration was opened at Corbelly Hill in 1884. The nuns also conducted a boarding school for young ladies which rapidly achieved a reputation as one of the foremost girls' public schools in Scotland. (Above) A group of pupils playing in the field in front of the Convent. (Below) Education was by no means confined to academic subjects, as this charming picture of a dancing class demonstrates.

ST ANDREW'S ATHLETIC FOOTBALL CLUB — A chapel dedicated to St Andrew was founded in 1811 to minister to the Roman Catholic families of Dumfries and Maxwelltown and a schoolroom was added in 1843. The School moved from Shakespeare Street in 1872 to Brooke Street. The boys were under the charge of the Marist Brothers, a teaching order noted for their muscular Christianity. Football was always a strongpoint of St Andrew's — hardly surprising as Brother Walfrid, founder of Glasgow Celtic FC, was among the teaching staff.

QUARRYMEN AT LOCHARBRIGGS — The red sandstone quarried on the outskirts of the town gives Dumfries its characteristically ruddy appearance, but this stone has been widely exported and provided the material for Glasgow's Kelvingrove Art Galleries and Museum, among many other impressive public buildings.

J.W. DODS, MONUMENTAL SCULPTOR — It is said of Sir Christopher Wren in St Paul's Cathedral 'If you want to see his monument, then look around you'. The same could be said of J.W. Dods whose tombstones and memorials are to be found in all the cemeteries of Dumfries; but this firm was also responsible for much of the architectural sculpture that adorns the public buildings of the town, from the town hall and the Ewart Library to the statuary on the Academy roof and the lions outside the Loreburn Hall.

MORRIN'S WHOLESALE FRUIT MARKET — R. & G. Morrin established their wholesale fruit warehouse in the New Market in Loreburn Street early in the 1880s. The picture shows barrels of Canadian apples and crates of Seville oranges, but in the gallery upstairs the firm had diversified into dairy produce from the farms of the surrounding district. This warehouse now forms the enclosed vehicle park of the police headquarters, while Morrin's are now located in the former Rosefield Mills in Troqueer.

HIRING FAIR AT THE MID STEEPLE — This practice by which farm servants were engaged by the half–year had been virtually unchanged since the Middle Ages. If things did not work out the farmworker could offer himself or herself at the next hiring fair. The hiring fair was also a great social occasion providing entertainment, sideshows and penny stalls. The buildings in this photograph are substantially the same today, although the names have changed.

FLOODING ON THE WHITESANDS — The building on the far right is the Coach and Horses Inn, a well–established hostelry in Burns's time, and haunt of the notorious prostitute Margaret Hog whom he immortalised in the rollicking ballad of Muirland Meg.

THE NITH IN FLOOD — The low-lying parts of the town have been prone to flooding for hundreds of years. Hardly a year goes by that a combination of high spring tides and the Nith in spate does not inundate the Whitesands, but in particularly severe cases the flood water has been known to advance across Nith Place and up Friars Vennel and Bank Street. Some of the worst flooding occurred on 2nd March 1910. In this general view the Whitesands area is completely under water, leaving only the retaining wall visible.

FLOODING AT THE MECHANICS' INSTITUTE — This photograph of Nith Place, viewed from the foot of Shakespeare Street, looks westward to the beginning of St Michael's Street. The 18th century town house of the Stuarts of Shambellie was acquired in 1825 for the Dumfries and Maxwelltown Mechanics' Institute and opened the following year. Members paid 8 shillings a year (children and apprentices only 4 shillings), but fifty years later the subscriptions were only half these amounts. In its heyday the Institute had 700 members, provided a wide range of lectures, an excellent reading room and a library of 8,000 volumes which was transferred to the Ewart Library in 1904. The Institute declined sharply after 1905 and was eventually converted into the Playhouse Cinema.

THE TOP OF NEWALL TERRACE — This view, taken in 1913, shows the narrow opening from Newall Terrace on to Loreburn Street, with its continuation into King Street over the rise. The buildings on the extreme left (now the Fleshers' Arms public house) still stand, but the buildings on the right were demolished as part of the street-widening process and were eventually replaced by the police station.

BEEHIVE CLOSE (left) — One of the narrow, cobbled closes running between Queensberry Square and Loreburn Street, it was among the first to be scheduled for demolition and redevelopment in the King Street Improvement Scheme of 1913. Work began soon afterwards but progress was held up by the outbreak of the First World War and a decade elapsed before the redevelopment of this congested area was completed.

SALE OF WORK — This photograph, taken in the summer of 1914, symbolises the end of an era which was soon to be swept away by the outbreak of the First World War. Ladies' hats were never so large or extravagant ever again. Third from the left in this group is Miss Jean Armour Burns Brown, last direct descendant of the poet to reside in Dumfries. Her large, expressive and penetrating eyes bore an uncanny resemblance to those of her famous great-grandfather.

DEPARTURE OF THE KOSB — The men of Maxwelltown and Troqueer march down Galloway Street, on their way to the drill hall in Newall Terrace.

TERRITORIALS MARCHING OFF TO WAR — The British Government declared war on Germany on 4th August 1914. A week later the Territorial battalions of the KOSB mustered in Dumfries and departed for active service. To the ever-recurring strains of 'Bonnie Gallowa', the Territorials march down Newall Terrace on their way to the railway station.

TROOPS AT THE RAILWAY STATION - Provost Thomas Macaulay bids farewell to the 2/5 Battalion KOSB outside the Station Hotel. Lieutenant-Colonel Sir Claude Laurie, DSO, the battalion commander (with plaid and stick), stands on the Provost's left.

THE WIDE ENTRY - This photograph was taken in 1915 shortly before these buildings on the east side of Queensberry Square were demolished to make way for Great King Street. The Wide Entry was the close on the extreme right (under the Robert Burns wine and spirit vaults) which provided access from the square to Loreburn Street. Lewthwaite's clog and clothing store (centre) closed down some time previously and was temporarily replaced by Stevenson's Rifle Range and Funland—the town's first amusement arcade.

ARROL JOHNSTON AIRCRAFT DIVISION - The motor industry of Dumfries began in 1907 when D. McKay Drummond built his first car at his brass foundry in Pleasance. This was never a commercial success and the company soon reverted to its more traditional operations as brass founders and pattern makers. In 1913, however, Arrol Johnston began production at Heathhall and later had a second factory at Tongland near Kirkcudbright. During the war this company diversified into aircraft production, as shown in this photograph taken in 1916.

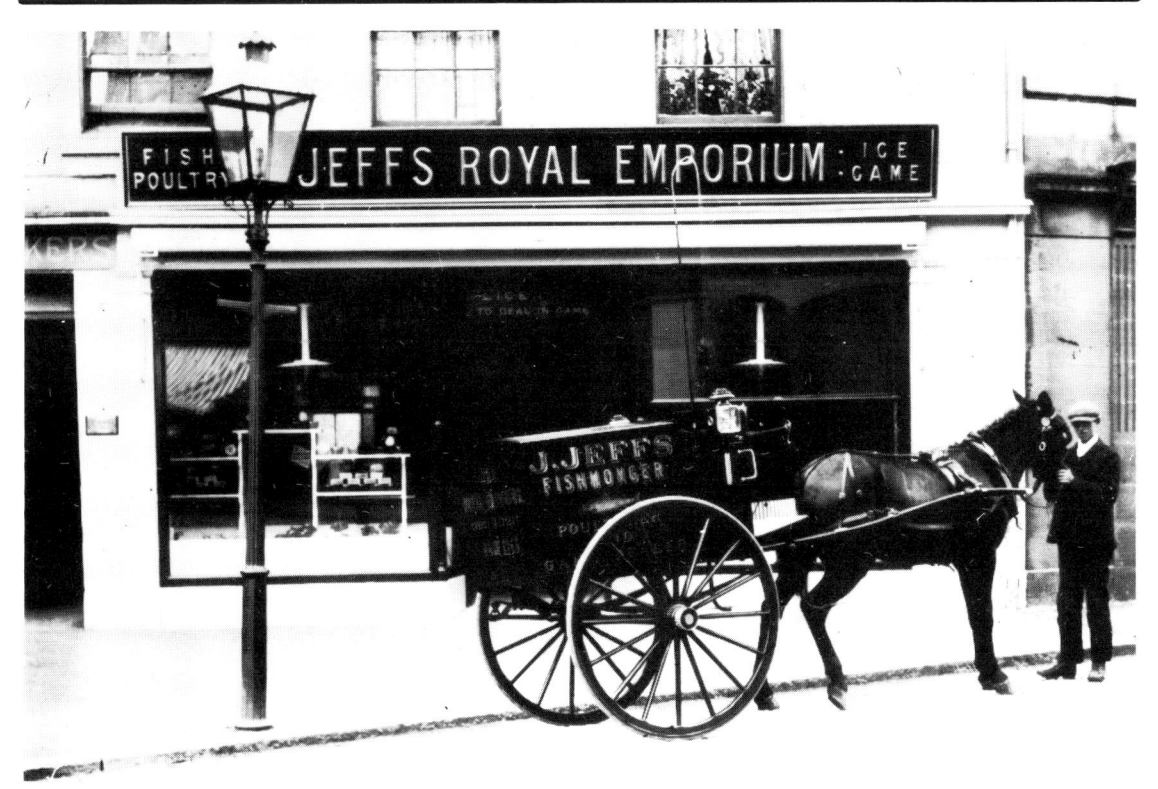

JEFFS' ROYAL EMPORIUM, CHURCH CRESCENT — This photograph dates from 1920 and shows the light cart drawn by a pony which was widely used by tradesmen until shortly before the Second World War. Jeffs the fishmonger was the father of Tim Jeffs, the illustrious sculptor, wood-carver and calligrapher who later operated the Yellow Door studio in Kirkcudbright.

THE HIGH STREET IN THE EARLY TWENTIES — The cobblestones had not yet given way to tarmac and there is a singular absence of motor traffic. Seiffert, the jeweller, became a casualty of the widespread Germanophobia of the War period and his premises at the Mid Steeple were now occupied by the Market Cross. The children are no longer barefoot, but the small shops have now given way to nationwide shops, insurance companies and building societies.

YOUTH MOVEMENTS — Organizations catering to young people began in 1883 with the Boys Brigade founded by William Smith of Glasgow and invariably linked to the (usually Presbyterian) church. The pill-boxes of the lads and the shakoes of their officers reflected the military uniform of the 1880s but continued until relatively recent years. (Above) This group shows the Dumfries BB with dummy rifles. Sir Robert Baden Powell founded the Scout movement in 1907 and his wife, Lady Olave, organized their female counterpart, the Girl Guides, a few years later. The 2nd Dumfries Guide Company (below) was attached to St John's Episcopal Church. The officers seated in the front row were Miss C. Walker, Miss Bullough (captain), Miss D.A. Pattie and Miss A. Waplington.

THE HORSE FAIR, 1922 — Some prewar customs continued for several years and the Horse Fair was still an important event, before the coming of the tractor and the motor vehicle. (Above) Circus ponies being watered in the Nith at the Sandy Opening. (Below) Clydesdale horses being paraded for sale. The 1922 Horse Fair, held in June, was dominated by William Johnstone of the Whitesands, who had 70 horses on offer, 'mostly seasoned animals, all fit for heavy work' which sold for up to £75 each.

THE ARROL JOHNSTON 15.9HP — This elegant convertible was the mainstay of the Dumfries motor industry in the immediate postwar period. Poor management and an inability to give the market what it wanted led to the decline of Arrol Johnston which went into liquidation in 1929.

CAR RALLY, 1923 — The cars in this photograph (from right to left) are a Rhodes, first registered in 1923 by Miss Janet Dickson Martin, a Humber, a Jowett, an Arrol Johnston built at Paisley before 1914 (identified by the radiator behind the bonnet) and an Arrol Johnston built at Dumfries in 1920–21.

PENMAN'S WORKSHOP — A.C. Penman began as a coach-builder, specialising in light carriages, but he was quick to see the potential of the internal combustion engine and built up a thriving business in the early years of this century. The first car body was constructed in 1902 and within three years the company's workshop in Queensberry Street was entirely devoted to this work. In 1908 Penman's moved to larger premises in St David Street (off Buccleuch Street) and concentrated on hand-built bodies (above). The firm became a limited company in 1928 and expanded under the chairmanship of James B. Penman, elder son of the founder. He died in 1954 and was succeeded by his brother John. As Penman Engineering Ltd., the company continues at Heathhall to this day. The group (below) shows the staff of Penman's in the early 1920s.

MOLLY MAXWELL — On 10th March 1924 Molly, the five year-old daughter of William and Eliza Maxwell, died. The grief-stricken parents commissioned a sculptor to carve a life-sized bas-relief of the little girl and this formed part of her tombstone. When it was erected in Troqueer churchyard it caused a sensation, and crowds flocked to see it. Those who had known Molly declared that the portrait was amazingly lifelike. In due course her parents were laid to rest in the same grave and their names were added to the tombstone.

THE VARSOPTIMISTS, 1928 — A group of Edinburgh University students, all former pupils of Dumfries Academy, who, during their vacations, toured their home county as entertainers. Included in the above picture are Duncan D. Brown, Alan Boyle, W. Bryson Grainger, Bella Park and Harold R. Armit.

GEORGE INN CLOSE — This photograph, taken in 1924, shows one of the slums in the town centre which were demolished soon afterwards when the area around Great King Street and Loreburn Street was redeveloped.

COUNCIL HOUSING — Dumfries was one of the pioneers of council housing, shortly before the First World War. In the postwar period the provision of substantial housing at economic rents was greatly expanded. Captain (later Colonel Sir) Walter Elliot, then Parliamentary Under Secretary for Health in the postwar Conservative government, laid the foundation stone of the Cresswell housing scheme on 23rd July 1923.

ST JOSEPH'S COLLEGE FOOTBALL TEAM, c.1922 — St Joseph's was founded in 1873 by the Marist Brothers and subsequently moved to St Michael's Mount. Under the able direction of Brother James it attracted pupils from all over the world and achieved a remarkable academic and sporting success in the earlier years of this century.

DEAD ELEPHANT ON THE WAY TO THE KNACKER'S YARD — Pinden's Circus was in Dumfries in 1923 when one of their elephants took ill and died. Firemen Bob McLachlan and Frank Scott were summoned to load the enormous carcase on to a Foden truck and cart it off to the knacker's yard.

LLOYD GEORGE AT DUMFRIES — The wartime Coalition premier visited the town in October 1925. On arrival at the railway station the VIPs posed for this picture: The young girl in the cloche and fur coat is Megan, LG's daughter—she was later to become a leading Labour MP. To her right are Dr Joseph Hunter, Dame Margaret Lloyd George, LG himself and, partly hidden by the latter, Randolph Dudgeon, Liberal MP for Galloway.

MAXWELLTOWN BOWLING CLUB, 1930 — Bowling as a pastime was well-established in the area centuries ago, but lawn bowling in its present form dates from the late 19th century. This group illustrates the inter-war fashions: most of the men, and all of the ladies, are hatted. The preponderance of ladies wearing fox-fur stoles is in sharp contrast with the present day trends, encouraged by animal rights activists, of wearing synthetic animal skins.

THE OPENING OF ST MICHAEL'S BRIDGE — Plans for a bridge linking Maxwelltown and Dumfries near the approach road to St Michael's Church were first considered in 1911 but were shelved for the duration of the war. The project was revived in the early 1920s and St Michael's Bridge was ceremonially opened in January 1927. (Above) the ceremony is shown from the Maxwelltown side, with the vast concourse lining the approach to Brooms Road in the background. (Below) The Duke of Buccleuch (Lord Lieutenant of Dumfriesshire) and the Sheriff of Dumfries and Galloway, Lord Kinross, being escorted to the Bridge.

ST MICHAEL'S BRIDGE CEREMONY — Provost Brodie of Maxwelltown, the Duke of Buccleuch, Provost O'Brien of Dumfries and the Town Clerk meeting at the centre of the Bridge.

THE BRITISH LEGION - Founded on behalf of the returned servicemen after the First World War, the Legion provides social and charitable amenities to this day. This group, taken in 1928, shows some of the early Dumfries members of the Legion: (standing) P.V. Fisher, W. Chalmers, George Wells, D. Jackson, J. Sheridan, J. Davidson, J. Smith, N. Dudson, J. Walker, J. Brown and S. Copland; (seated) J. Wilson, Lieut. Colonel Mathers DSO, OBE, DCM, J. Beck, Major W. Wilson DSO, MC, Lieut. Colonel William Robertson, VC, OBE, JP, J. Bryden, Lieut. Colonel H.F. Blair Imrie CMG, OBE and H. Kerr. Colonel Robertson, a native of Dumfries, won his Victoria Cross as a sergeant-major in the Gordon Highlanders at Elandslaagte and received a battlefield commission. He suffered the hardships of the siege of Ladysmith but on his return home, on 24th December 1900, was given the freedom of the burgh.

CHILDREN'S ROUNDABOUT — The first recreational amenity for children to be erected in Dumfries was this cast-iron roundabout, placed in the Long Close between High Street and Irish Street in 1935. This area was subsequently redeveloped and the roundabout transferred to the Dock Park.

MRS GOLOGLY — Mary Gologly was one of the town's more kenspeckle figures in the interwar period. A very stout figure, invariably dressed in black, she presided over a junk shop beside the Rainbow Stairs. The lady with the shopping basket is her close friend, Mrs Vernon. The sign 'Licensed Broker' above the door indicates that she was permitted to deal in such commodities as silver and animal skins, in addition to her trade in secondhand clothing, furniture and crockery. Mrs Gologly's emporium was located on the site of Burton's near the Mid Steeple.

WAR MEMORIAL, MAXWELLTOWN — Memorials to the fallen of previous wars were confined to discreet plaques on the walls of parish churches, but the carnage of the First World War was on such a horrendous scale that something more public was demanded. Both Dumfries and Maxwelltown lost no time in erecting granite or bronze statues on tall pedestals inscribed with the names of their war dead. The Maxwelltown statue, at the corner of Rotchell and New Abbey Roads, was unveiled in November 1920, on the second anniversary of the Armistice.

TITANIC MEMORIAL — The world's largest liner, the White Star *Titanic* left Southampton on her maiden voyage for New York on 10th April 1912. Four days later, at 11.40p.m., she collided with an iceberg and sank two and a half hours later. The loss of life was appalling and few towns were untouched by the tragedy. John Law Hume and Thomas Mullin, natives of Dumfries and Maxwelltown, went down with the ship. An obelisk (left) in the Dock Park was erected in their memory.

IN MEMORY OF
JOHN LAW HUME, A MEMBER OF THE BAND
AND THOMAS MULLIN, STEWARD,
NATIVES OF THESE TOWNS
WHO LOST THEIR LIVES IN THE WRECK OF
THE WHITE STAR LINER "TITANIC"
WHICH SANK IN MID-ATLANTIC
ON THE 14TH DAY OF APRIL 1912.
THEY DIED AT THE POST OF DUTY

YOUNG LOCHINVAR — George Shirley wrote plays and pageants which were staged as part of the early Guid Nychburris festivals. In this performance of the Border romance 'Young Lochinvar' the eponymous hero was played by a Mr Mulholland. The other parts were played by (left to right) Jean Thomson, Gordon Maxwell, Mabel Welsh, Willie Chisholm, Fergus Waugh, Norman Brodie, Grace Laurie, Edith Waugh, Lewis Beattie, Spence Culbert and Molly Duncan. Grace Laurie was the sister of John Laurie, the Shakespearian actor and veteran of many films but perhaps best remembered as Private Fraser of the TV series 'Dad's Army'.

THE HIGH STREET LOOKING NORTH — The Burns statue and Greyfriars Church can be seen in the background. In this photograph of 1930 the cobblestones have been replaced by tarmac and a few motor vehicles are now in evidence. The 'flappers' are wearing skirts that barely reach the knee, but older women continue to wear the ankle-length fashions of the Edwardian era. The Steeple Tea Rooms (near left) were a favourite meeting place in the Twenties.

THE RAINBOW STAIRS, 1930 — Originally the burgh tolbooth in the 15th century, this structure was substantially rebuilt in 1718 as a council chamber approached by the flight of stairs over a small lock-up where malefactors were lodged while awaiting trial. The council moved to more commodious premises about 1832 and the building became the Rainbow Tavern. Later it was converted into shops and offices, such as the Magneto Accumulator Electro-plating Company whose main business was recharging wet-cell batteries for the early wireless sets.

THE PENTHOUSE END — This was the gate-house at the southeastern extremity of the medieval town, at the end of St Michael's Street, and a much-loved landmark, even if it had been allowed to become rather dilapidated. Fortunately when it was demolished in 1931 it was replaced by a sandstone building of traditional style. The buildings on the extreme right, however, were demolished to provide wider access to Burns Street.

RIDING THE MARCHES — In common with many Border towns, Dumfries had an annual ceremony of riding the marches or burgh boundaries but the custom fell into disuse as written records became more commonplace. This ceremony was revived in 1932 by George Shirley the burgh librarian as part of a package of events rather quaintly named Guid Nychburris (good neighbours) Week. Considerable controversy raged over this Old Scots expression but it is now well entrenched. The photograph of 1937 shows Cornet George McKerrow (in top hat) and his escorts at the cemetery gates.

THE MUNICIPAL ORCHESTRA — Between the wars Dumfries boasted a fine municipal orchestra. This picture was taken on 20th March 1934 when the Orchestra took part in a programme broadcast in the Scottish Regional Service of the BBC. (Standing) J.P. Lockhart, G. Stewart, W. Adams, W. McC. Blair, George Percy, S. Hales, T. Barnes, F. Clark, J. Kerr and C. McNulty; (middle row) F.D. Smith, Miss F. Mackie, A. Shepherd, J. Marshall, J. Tinning, A. Brooker, W. Ashton, Miss A. Hannay, J. Marshall junr.; (front row) Miss H. Keddie, Miss Grace Laurie, Mrs Kerr (leader), James Blair (conductor), Mrs J.W. Pirie, Miss M. Hannay and Miss L. Graham.

ROYAL VISIT — The first Royal Visit since James VI presented theSiller Gun in 1617 occurred on 20th September 1932 when HRH the Duke of Gloucester came to Dumfries. He is shown here, accompanied by Provost Brodie, in St Michael's Churchyard after visiting the Burns Mausoleum.

BRITISH LINEN BANK — Erected in 1934 at the corner of Great King Street and Queensberry Street, it is now a branch of the Bank of Scotland. The photograph shows the building nearing completion — only the dome is not quite finished. At the same time, work on the Imperial Restaurant across the street was well under way, to judge by the sign on the builder's hoarding. In the Seventies the latter site was semi-derelict for a number of years and was an eyesore, but it has subsequently been renovated.

DUMFRIES AND GALLOWAY NATURAL HISTORY AND ANTIQUARIAN SOCIETY — This august body of savants was founded in 1862 and has since played a leading role in the development and maintenance of the Burgh Museum as well as publishing its valuable *Transactions* The photograph shows a group of the Antiquarians on a summer excursion. On the extreme left is the MP for the Stewartry. Third from the left is the eminent historian, Sir Herbert Maxwell.

STAFF OF THE DUMFRIES AND GALLOWAY STANDARD — Founded in 1843 as a radical newspaper by the Rev. Dr. Henry Duncan, it continued in the Liberal tradition till the 1920s but then veered to the right under the proprietorship of the Misses Watson who were staunch Conservatives. The staff in 1933 were (left to right) Bryce Craig, Eddie Whitehead, W.G. Muir (Editor), David Dunbar and John Ritchie.

QUEENSBERRY SQUARE — This photograph of March 1934 was taken from the offices of the *Dumfries and Galloway Standard* shortly before the Queensberry monument was moved to the County Buildings and the underground public lavatory behind it was demolished. By that time these landmarks were proving a hazard to the burgeoning traffic. The cobblestones were replaced by tarmac shortly afterwards. The Linen Bank was absorbed by the Bank of Scotland in 1971. The building behind it, further up Great King Street, was the head post office, opened in 1926. The site further up was redeveloped as an extension to the post office in 1963. The Foresters' Arms and adjoining shops were later swallowed up in the bank expansion of the 1980s.

SUSPENSION BRIDGE, 1936 — For the convenience of the millworkers living in Gasstown but employed by the Troqueer and Rosefield Mills, this iron suspension foot-bridge was erected in 1872-75. In the left foreground is the park near the present-day Burns Centre (formerly the old Town Mill).

BLACKSHIRTS ON PARADE — Sir Oswald Mosley's British Union of Fascists were spawned by the Depression and even Dumfries—a town which seldom espoused extremes in politics—had its quota of Fascist paramilitaries. The historian Alfred Truckell has recorded that when Mosley addressed a noisy meeting in the Drill Hall his storm-troopers clubbed hecklers senseless with the steel balls on chains round their wrists but the police did not intervene. The photograph shows the dedication of Fascist banners at a parade in Friars Vennel.

GIRDERS IN CHAOS - This spectacular mess was created during the re-roofing of the Lyceum Cinema. Unfortunately the structure was overstressed and collapsed on 16th July 1936.

MILITARY MANOEUVRES — The troops in this photograph of 1940 are wearing British uniforms and equipment and firing British Lee-Enfield rifles and a Bren light machine gun - but they are, in fact, Poles engaged in manoeuvres with Norwegians. Dumfries and district provided a temporary home for exiled Europeans.

RESCUE SQUAD — On the outbreak of the Second World War in September 1939 there were fears that the country would be subjected to widespread aerial bombardment and gas attacks. Air Raid Precautions began as early as 1935 and ARP sections were rapidly mobilised. The men in this group, dating from 1940, are identified as rescue workers from the initial R on their steel helmets. The haversacks slung over the chest, would contain Service respirators.

KING HAAKON VII IN DUMFRIES — The town became the wartime headquarters of the Free Norwegian Forces. In 1940 King Haakon came to Dumfries to inspect his troops. The King is shown arriving by train, accompanied by British staff officers.

NORGES HUS — Oughton's Restaurant, opposite Burns Statue, became the wartime headquarters of the Norwegian forces and was temporarily renamed Norges Hus (Norway's House). The Scottish-Norwegian Society was formed to provide the troops with social amenities and home comforts. Provost John Lockerbie is introduced to Norwegian girls during an exhibition staged in 1941; Major Olaus Myrseth (in service dress and riding boots) looks on. The Swastika above the door is on the tail-fin of a wrecked Nazi fighter plane.

THE WAR IS OVER — Provost Ernest Fyfe reads the proclamation announcing the cessation of hostilities in the Far East on VJ Day, 1st September 1945—six years to the day since Nazi troops invaded Poland. Contrast this rather subdued scene with the 1902 scene on page 51. The area below the stairs was still used as a shop (tobacconist's), but the Electricity Board now had their showrooms on the other side of the Mid Steeple. Maxwell's stationery shop was now renamed Dinwiddie's. Very few of the women in the crowd are now wearing hats.

DUMFRIES GIRLS' CHOIR — E.A. Whitehead, Music Organiser for the County and founder of the Girls' Choir, is shown conducting an impromptu concert in 1951.

CARNATION MILK FACTORY, 1950 — This plant, for the processing of milk products, especially evaporated milk, was introduced in 1934-35 and located near Lincluden on the west bank of the Nith. It was considerably expanded in the immediate postwar years and remains one of the principal employers in the town.

ICI PLASTICS FACTORY, 1950 — Imperial Chemical Industries constructed a factory at Drungans on the western outskirts of the town in 1938-39 for the manufacture of high explosives. After the Second World War ICI built a new factory alongside for the production of Ardil, a synthetic fibre from groundnut waste. This project was a victim of the great Groundnut Fiasco but the factory was converted to the manufacture of plastic film and this has subsequently expanded very considerably.

SCISSORS GRINDER IN THE HIGH STREET — Once a common sight, the itinerant grinder of knives and scissors (shown here about 1950) is now a thing of the past.

BURNS STATUE, C.1950 — The building immediately behind the poet's statue was the original Episcopal church and is now derelict. The Stead & Simpson shoe shop on the extreme left stood near the sight of the original Greyfriars where Bruce slew the Comyn.

CASTLE STREET, 1951 — The buildings in Castle Street were developed in the early 19th century and retain their Regency elegance to this day. The photograph looks eastwards towards McCall's Corner at the top of Buccleuch Street.

SENIOR STAFF OF THE INFIRMARY, 1954 — (Back row) Miss I.K. Thorburn (Home Sister), J. Brownless (Board Secretary) and Miss E.L.R. Johnstone (Assistant Matron); (front row) Matron J.K. Hutt and Miss Margaret Steenson. Miss Steenson was born in 1872, trained as a nurse at the Infirmary and served in the Boer War, ultimately becoming a matron in Queen Alexandra's Royal Army Nursing Corps (QARANC). The photograph was taken on the occasion of Miss Steenson's visit to her old training hospital.

IS IT ANIMAL, VEGETABLE OR MINERAL? — In 1953 Dumfries played host to a National Archaeological Conference. Messrs Wainright, Powell and Kennedy are shown here with John Clark, Professor Stuart Piggott and Sir Mortimer Wheeler. The two lastnamed achieved celebrity through the popular television programme 'Animal, Vegetable or Mineral' which brought archaeology before a wide audience in the Fifties.

ST JOHN'S EPISCOPAL CHURCH CHOIR — This photograph, taken in 1952, shows the organist E. Murray on the left and the Curate, the Rev. J. McClure, on the extreme right.

THE ROYAL HIGHLAND SHOW, 1954 — The Royal Highland and Agricultural Society's annual show is now a permanent fixture at Ingliston, but until the end of the 1950s it was a peripatetic event. In recent years it had been held at Dumfries in 1930 and 1938 and was last staged in the town in June 1954. On that occasion the Show was visited by Her Majesty Queen Elizabeth, the Queen Mother. (Above) Heavy rain did not mar the occasion for the large crowds which attended. (Below) The Queen Mother later signed the Distinguished Visitors' Book in the Municipal Chambers. On her right stands Provost George H. Mogerley and on her left is James Hutcheon, the Town Clerk. On the wall behind can be seen the portraits of two previous provosts, Thomas Macaulay and James McGeorge.

AUTUMN INUNDATION — Incessant rain over the weekend of 15th–17th October 1954 resulted in unprecedented flooding, causing widespread damage. On this occasion many of the roads in the surrounding district were impassable to motor traffic, particularly the Dumfries–Castle Douglas road at Shawhead and the Collin Road where the Lochar Water burst its banks. Bystanders watching the Nith in spate from the Old Bridge (above) were horrified when a young man toppled over the parapet and was swept off to his death. He had clambered over the top to get a better view and lost his footing.

BILLY HOULISTON —Queen of the South F.C. was formed in 1919 out of the former Dumfries, KOSB and Arrol-Johnston clubs. After a period in limbo (1939-45) Queens were reconstituted and got off to a good start by thrashing Hibs 3-0. In September 1945 Billy Houston joined the team at outside right, and scored one of the goals that gave Queen's their 4-1 victory over Celtic that month. Houliston went on to become a bye-word in Scottish football and in his heyday Palmerston Park was a Mecca for Soccer fans. In 1949 Billy was chosen to play for Scotland against England at Wembley—the first South of Scotland player to have this honour. The game resulted in a 3–1 victory for Scotland with Billy unsettling the English defence and driving them to the point of desperation. In 1952 Billy was transferred to Berwick Rangers.

WHITESANDS, 1955 — The tinkers' camps are now long gone, their place taken by the buses of Western SMT whose offices are on the left foreground. Across the road is the waiting room, with the Old Bridge and Town Mill (now the Burns Centre) beyond. In the middle distance is the Mill Green and the Suspension and St Michael's Bridges. On the horizon (left) is the spire of the church of the Crichton Royal Institution. On the left are the Lyceum and St Michael's Church, with the old Infirmary beyond and the Craigs rising up to the left.

THE OLD BRIDGE HOUSE — The oldest house in Maxwelltown is the cottage that stands at the end of the Old Bridge. Now a museum, it was still occupied as a dwelling in the 1950s. There are a clutter of outhouses and a tiny privy at the rear of the building overlooking the wall above the river bank. The Bridge itself was still cobbled; in more recent times a protective layer of tarmac was laid on top.

GUID NYCHBURRIS, c.1955 — The Town Band, provost and burgh officers escort the dismounted Cornet, Cornet's Lass, lynors, bailies, magistrates and councillors at the commencement of the week-long festivities.

THE TOWN BAND, c.1955 — The municipal brass band leads the procession from the Municipal Chambers in Buccleuch Street, along the High Street, past the Mid Steeple and Binns department store, on the way to the church service known as Kirkin' the Cornet in St Michael's. Binns, one of the old established department stores, closed down in August 1990.

ST JOHN'S CHURCH, 1958 — The Episcopal Church of St John the Evangelist, to give it its full name, replaced an earlier church (at the corner of Castle and Buccleuch Streets) which had been used from 1820. The foundation stone of St John's was laid on 1st August 1867. The site, at the corner of Newall Terrace and Lovers' Walk, is well fitted to set off the massive form and bold details of the Gothic design, topped by a spire 40 metres in height. The church was consecrated on 3rd December 1868.

TRAVELLING SUPPORT — These enthusiastic supporters were on their way to watch the Academy team play Lanark Grammar in the replay of the Scottish Secondary Schools Shield. As with the final itself this encounter ended in a 1–1 draw. Dumfries were unlucky to lose the second replay 2–1 to a goal scored four minutes before the end of extra time. The School's results over the preceding four years had been remarkable—winners in 1956, quarter finalists 1957, semi finalists 1958 and beaten finalists 1959— despite these being the only competitive football matches the team played.

SWIMMING IN THE NITH — The unusually hot summer of 1955 encouraged bathers who flocked to the Nith just below the Caul.

AERIAL PHOTOGRAPH OF DUMFRIES FROM THE SOUTH — In the foreground can be seen the vast textile mills which were then still in full production, Troqueer and Rosefield on the left and Nithsdale Mills on the right. Characteristically, the Nith is in flood again, and the extent of the inundation can be seen on the Whitesands and the approach to the Dock Park, with the road from St Michael's Bridge virtually impassable. Beyond the four bridges can be seen the roofs of the vast postwar council housing estates of Lincluden and Lochside.

ENGLISH STREET, 1956 — This picture (above), taken from the corner of Shakespeare Street, looks up the street towards Loreburn Street. While the building on the left-hand corner was being erected in 1897 there came to light one of the public draw-wells once so common in Dumfries. About 7 metres deep and a metre in diameter, the well was faced halfway down with stone and for the remaining depth with brick. The houses on the right, beyond the first of the motor vehicles, were erected about the same time, hence the name Jubilee Mansions (alluding to Queen Victoria's Diamond Jubilee of 1897). The much earlier picture below shows English Street from the corner of Loreburn Street. On the left foreground stand the Jubilee Buildings with a sculptured bust of Queen Victoria clearly visible in a niche on the first storey.

SHAKESPEARE STREET (LOWER END), 1958 — The building on the extreme right foreground is Roan's barber-shop at the foot of the Southergate. The site was redeveloped in 1960 and now, thirty years on, it is being developed again, this time to provide a shopping mall. Ney's the watchmaker (opposite) was swallowed up in an earlier phase of redevelopment which resulted in a vast Presto supermarket, now superseded by Safeway. *Sic transit gloria mundi* It was feared that the building in the background would also be demolished in the 1960s, but miraculously it has survived. Originally the home of Archibald Malcolm, Town Clerk of Dumfries, which he built for himself in 1753, it is now the headquarters of the Royal British Legion.

HIGH STREET, 1957 — The postcard (above), looking towards Greyfriars Church, shows the shops that existed before the department stores and building societies began to take over. Of the shops on the left, only Johnstone the grocer survived to the 1970s. Spence Culbert's pharmacy, Greta Humphrey's china shop and other once-familiar shops have long since vanished from the scene. Woolworth's were the first of the national chain stores to get a foothold on the High Street. Milligan's bakery has also gone. One by one the familiar shops with their weel-kent names above the doors have disappeared, and with them has gone all (except the Mid steeple itself) that distinguished the High Street of Dumfries from other high streets the length and breadth of Britain.

SOUTHERGATE BRAE, 1958 — The southern end of the High Street was in decay by the time this photograph was taken. The small shops (left to right)—Hutchison the clogger, Inman the baker, Roan the barber and Appleton, who doubled as tobacconist and pawnbroker—were allowed to fall into disrepair, prior to demolition and redevelopment in the 1980s.

ROBERT CARRUTHERS MINERAL WATER WORKS—The town was formerly noted for the purity of the water drawn from deep artesian wells. Those sunk below the premises of Robert Carruthers in Newall Terrace were the most elaborate and attained a depth of about 120 metres. This mineral water served as the basis for the range of soft drinks purveyed by this company. The firm went out of business in 1960 and the buildings were demolished to make way for a carpark serving the County Buildings. The site is now occupied by an extension to the Regional offices, completed in 1990.

GUID NYCHBURRIS — The Cornet, Lass and Pursuivant emerge from the Wee Vennel (now Bank Street) and head for the Mid Steeple for the presentation of the Burgh Charter.

THE ROOD FAIR BY NIGHT, 1960 — The homespun quality of the prewar Rood Fairs gave way to the glitter and glamour of the postwar professional fair circuits. Even after dark the fairground was an exciting spectacle, with its neon lights and festoons of bright bulbs. Women are now bareheaded but skirts are at the fashionable mid-calf length, a contrast with the austerity of the immediate postwar years.

CORNET AND QUEEN OF THE SOUTH — The dismounted Cornet escorts the Queen of the South from the dais at the Mid Steeple. The Provost and Cornet's escorts look on in the background.

COACH AND HORSES INN — Once a common sight in Dumfries, the decorated gipsy wagon, drawn by a pony, was a rarity by 1960 when this photograph was taken.

STEAM LOCOMOTIVE — In 1962 a group of railway enthusiasts organised a tour of Scotland using a steam locomotive. Steampower was phased out in the late 1950s and replaced by diesels and electric trains.

DUMFRIES STATION SIGNAL TOWER - This polygonal tower with its mock crenellated battlements was erected by the Caledonian Railway Company in 1863 at the opening of their line between Dumfries and Lockerbie, via Lochmaben. The line closed in May 1964 and the tower was allowed to fall into disrepair, though it was not actually demolished until 3rd November 1971.

BOATING IN THE VENNEL — In January 1962 the Nith burst its banks yet again. The flooding was so severe that, for a time, the only way to get along Friars Vennel and the streets running at right angles from it was by boat.

FRIARS VENNEL — Running from the north end of the High Street to the Whitesands, this was always one of the busiest shopping streets of the town. Its shopkeepers and tradesmen supplied the wants of a wide community, and there was a warm neighbourliness among all who lived and worked there. The Vennel was particularly lively during the March and Rood Fairs when many of the sideshows spilled over from the Sands. Then the Vennel became 'a Klondyke for the fiddlers, melodeon-players and singers that followed the Fair,' as Ex-Provost Mogerley (long-time butcher in the Vennel) has described it fondly.

DUMFRIES MALE VOICE CHOIR — This group, taken in 1971, shows the choir on the stage of Dumfries Academy. The ornamental organ screen in the background was carved by Tim Jeffs, a local artist, wood-carver and sculptor of considerable ability.

KING OLAV V OF NORWAY — On 19th October 1962 King Olav V of Norway returned to Dumfries to receive the Freedom of the Burgh and renew wartime contacts. He is shown here being presented to local dignitaries at the Lyceum Cinema.

RUSSIAN DELEGATION - In November 1986 a delegation of the Russian Federation of Labour toured Dumfries and paid a visit to the Robert Burns Centre, which had recently been inaugurated in the former Town Mill. The group shows (left to right) Vladislav Tsarey, David Lockwood (Curator of the Nithsdale District Museums), Provost Ken Cameron, Vladimir Fomenko and Roy Watson (Chairman of Leisure and Recreation) on the balcony overlooking the Nith.

THE FOUNTAIN, 1970 — This scene, where English Street meets the High Street, has changed considerably in the past two decades. On the left stands the venerable King's Arms Hotel, a listed building of considerable architectural and historic merit. Alongside are buildings dating back to Burns's time. Both were allowed to decay beyond the point of no return and were pulled down in 1979. Miraculously the building next to them (above Muir's hairdressing salon) was saved and has since been beautifully restored. Just round the corner is the entrance to the Globe Inn, Burns's favourite howff. Note the clutter of parked cars on the street and the one-way system in English Street.

NITHSDALE MILLS — These photographs, taken in January 1990, show the vast complex of the Nithsdale textile mills immediately prior to their demolition. Like some enormous Gothic bastion, the Mills were one of the town's most prominent landmarks. In the post-industrial revival of Dumfries the site, alongside St Michael's Street, is now of greater value for housing and office accommodation.

DUMFRIES HIGH SCHOOL — Opened in 1961 as a Junior High School, its most academically gifted pupils transferred to the Academy at the end of the second year. This practice changed in the 1980s when the school became a comprehensive and therefore able to cater for the educational needs of all secondary school age pupils. The picture above shows the first sixth year class to have completed their entire secondary education at Dumfries High School.

CHAMPIONS OF SCOTLAND — The Hampden Squad 1984. Back row; A Sorrel, S Williamson, M Fleming, B Crosbie, D Purdie, D McHenry, M Pattison, D Clark. Front row; J Shankland, M Blount, W Cross, I Jardine, G Muir, D McAllister. Winners of the Esso Scottish Secondary Schools Shield 1984. By beating Columba High School of Coatbridge 2–0, at Hampden Park on 2nd June 1984, Dumfries Academy under–18 side repeated their great victory of 1956 and thus gave their Principal Teacher of P.E. the perfect retiral gift. Since arriving at the Academy in 1954 Lachie Campbell had been the driving force behind the team's campaigns.

COMMONWEALTH CHAMPION — For many years a member of Dumfries Bowling Club, Denis Love has been Club champion five times between 1979 and 1990, a Scottish internationalist in 1979-83 and 1989-90. Champion of Champions in 1980, a decade later he was a member of the Scottish rink which won the Gold Medal at the Commonwealth Games in Auckland. The four members of the rink were; George Adrain, Ian Bruce, Denis Love and skip Willie Wood.

SCOTTISH BADMINTON CHAMPION — Anne Gibson started playing badminton at the age of 8 and four times won Scottish National Junior titles, before going on to win the Senior singles title (1989-90). Ranked Number One woman player in Scotland, she gained the Bronze in the European Junior Championships—the only Scot ever to win a singles medal in any European Championship. At the World Championship in Indonesia (1989) Anne won all her singles matches. She repeated this feat at the European Championships in Moscow (1990) and in so doing helped the Scottish team to gain promotion to Division One in European badminton.

ANNE GIBSON
SCOTTISH INTERNATIONAL BADMINTON PLAYER

CRICHTON HALL — Dr. James Crichton of Friars' Carse left his fortune to such charitable purposes as his widow should choose. A plan for a University was rejected; instead Mrs. Crichton founded the lunatic asylum which is now known as the Crichton Royal Hospital and opened in 1839. It rapidly attained pre-eminence as the foremost institution in the world for the study of mental illness, a position it enjoys to this day.

DUMFRIES AND GALLOWAY ROYAL INFIRMARY — In 1990 Dumfries was judged to be the best place to live in Scotland (and second only to Nottingham, nationwide). Undoubtedly the outstanding qualities of health care, epitomised in the DGRI, played a large part in this judgement. Opened by the Queen on 4th July 1975, it cost over £5 million, has 424 beds and a staff of over 400.